THE WINNING MANAGER

THE WINNING MANAGER

Coming Out on Top
in the Organisation Game

Reggie von Zugbach

SOUVENIR PRESS

First published 1995 by Souvenir Press Ltd, 43 Great Russell Street, London WC1B 3PA and simultaneously in Canada

ISBN 0 285 63209 4

Phototypeset by Intype, London
Printed and bound in Great Britain by
Mackays of Chatham PLC, Chatham, Kent

Contents

Acknowledgements   ix

To the Winning Manager   1

1 The Organisation Game   3

2 The Enemy Within   22

3 Joined Up Enemies   44

4 Organisations as Your Enemy   71

5 The Winning Agenda   94

6 Buying Souls   120

7 Leaders Win   152

Notes and References   188

Index   193

TO NOBODY

*You are on your own
and you had better learn this now!*

Acknowledgements

How often have you seen organisations and the people who inhabit them stifle creative managers while seeming to nurture the mediocre, the stupid and even the incompetent? Certainly, I have observed this over a spectrum of experience that includes finance, publishing, the drinks industry, information technology, the government service and education. I thank all those who have, albeit inadvertently, contributed to making this book possible. I hope my students can benefit from what I have seen.

I would sincerely thank my publishers for their motivating encouragement, their creative suggestions, their patience and even their gentle bullying during the writing of this book, marred as it was by a disastrous loss of the first draft through IT systems failure (my excuse for technical incompetence).

My best thanks must go to Sarah Dougan, without whom the book would not have been written at all. Without her help, I would not have picked up the pieces after the disaster. She has not only edited my ideas but has made a major contribution to the delivery of them. Sarah, THANK YOU!

R.v.Z.
Paisley, 1995

To the Winning Manager

My aim in writing this book is to transform you into a new manager who will be a winner in the organisation game. Perhaps the narrow-minded among you will dismiss my views as heresy because you have been brainwashed into accepting a status quo which has moulded you into an 'organisation' man or woman. Yet has the status quo given you what you want? Hasn't it left you feeling tired, frustrated and unsuccessful? Do you look on your career with enthusiasm, or do you describe it as 'the grindstone', 'the treadmill' or 'just a job'? I want to show you management techniques that will enable you to take control of your life and gain power in the organisation; but they will only succeed if you also adopt winner's ways of thinking.

Your first step must be to abandon the conventional attitudes that have held you back, and to replace them with a new set of rules, based on the following Winner's Commandments:

1 Me first. Nobody else will put your interests before theirs.
2 There are no absolute rules. Other people's ideas of right and wrong do not apply to you.
3 The organisation is there to serve your interests, not the other way round.
4 You are on your own. Nobody is going to help you become a winner.
5 Be paranoic. Watch out, the bastards *are* out to get you.
6 Suck up to those who matter and suck up well. Identify the key people in the system who will help you.
7 Say one thing and do another. You need to pay lip-

service to the organisation's cherished notions of how things should be done.

8   Be a team-player, but make sure you beat your fellow team members.

9   Remember that the truth is not always to your advantage. Those who control your future do not necessarily want to hear the bad news.

10 Manipulate the facts to suit your interests. Even when things are bad you should come up smelling of roses.

11 Get your retaliation in first. When there is blood on the organisation's carpet, make sure it's not yours.

12 Blow your own trumpet—or better still, get someone else to do it for you.

13 Dominate your environment or it will dominate you.

Keep these guidelines before you at all times. Memorise them, practise them, become so familiar with them that you follow their precepts automatically. They are the key to your success in the organisation game.

1 The Organisation Game

For most of us, organisations represent the means by which we gain our livelihood and are the sole outlets for our creative energies. Surely the serious business of earning a living or attempting to fulfil oneself is far too important to be trivialised as a game?

Consider, however, the mass of books on the subject of the management of organisations: they are full of the terminology of the games field. They speak of strategies and tactics, of attack and defence, even of 'beating the socks off the opposition'.[1] Managerial life clearly is a game in that it creates winners and losers. Look around you in your own company. You will quickly be able to identify the winners, those who have succeeded in gaining power in the organisation, and their counterparts, the losers—the failures, the embittered, those who could or should have done better but who somehow came last in the struggle for dominance.

There is nothing new in this idea. More than forty years ago Stephen Potter,[2] in his humorous classic *One-Upmanship*, portrayed the world of human interaction as a complex game in which individuals could use any number of moves to win advantage over their fellows. On a more serious note, Eric Berne's seminal *Games People Play*[3] showed how human interaction could be understood by reference to a set of moves with pay-offs for individuals. Berne argued that people behave in ways that offer the best advantage over others. They will naturally try to achieve their own ends, to become winners. The life of the manager is no different, in this respect, from any other form of human activity. The outcome that managers seek is power over their managerial lives and, therefore, power in the organisation.

Of course, the traditional view of management does not prescribe the pursuit of self-interest. Instead it recommends that we become conscientious team-players. Pick up any conventional book on management and, right from the first page, you will be addressed as though certain assumptions were taken for granted:

- As a manager, you want the best for the enterprise in which you work.
- You will comply with its ways of doing things in order to make it more successful.
- You will subordinate your aims, your desires, your personality, even your life, to the perceived greater good of the organisation.
- You will take on the mantle of the 'Organisation Man'[4] and play to win—for the organisation.
- You will be a willing victim in this process, which is in effect the purchase of your soul, in return for a salary, security, status and perhaps even the trappings of power.

Most managers succumb to this way of thinking, to their own detriment. All around you are intelligent, strong people who have been made mindless and weak by their attachment to the organisation's team, on the organisation's terms. Nowhere, in the serious literature of management or in the training of managers, are these assumptions questioned. Nor is there any encouragement for managers to pursue their own self-interest.

The reasons for this are obvious. Writers and teachers on management are, after all, part of a system which rewards them for producing compliant and conscientious men and women. Even if they considered alternative roles for managers in organisations, it would not be in their interest to promote them. But there are other ways of approaching managerial life, as I shall show you.

The propaganda message of conventional management training is that managers who are assimilated into the culture of the organisational 'team', and learn to play the organisation game for the interests of the organisation, will prosper. This may be true. Organisational virtue tends to reap its reward—eventually—but the process is a long-term one and has no guarantee of success. The tactics described in this book are calculated to achieve the same results more quickly and with a much higher success rate. They do, however, require a substantial input from two qualities which never enter the vocabulary of existing management gurus: cynicism and selfishness. Expressed in psychological terms, the winning manager needs to develop the traits of paranoia and psychopathy. If you want to be a winner in the organisation game you must play for yourself and yourself alone.

Before all you propagandists and conventional theorists issue a veto on this book for fear that it will induce mass revolt in your organisations, answer the following. Would you describe Henry Ford, Lord Hanson, Rupert Murdoch and Bill Gates as compliant organisation men who accepted the status quo? Or would you describe them as winners who injected industry with the insulin it so desperately required? If the latter, read on.

Those who are still not convinced by my argument should consider the work of Karl von Clausewitz (1780–1831), a German army officer of humble origin, who rose to high rank in the Russian and Prussian armies.[5] He was noted for his ability to see how traditional management had failed the armies that had to confront the revolutionary military methods of Napoleon. In his book *On War* he designed a model for officer training in the Prussian army, which was so successful that it is still used in military establishments and among some of the more enlightened commercial organisations all over the world. He argued that there are four types of manager:

Shrewd and hardworking. These tend to be specialists and experts. Clausewitz made them staff officers who could devote their intelligence to ensuring that the rations reached the troops and that enough ammunition was available. They are 'systems' people. In modern organisations they are represented by experts and 'back room boys'.

Simple and lazy. These people are too stupid to disobey orders. They will do exactly what you want, no more and no less. There are plenty of jobs for them in the army and modern organisations, where they are represented by line managers.

Simple and hardworking. These are a common type in both organisations and the army. They will grab any task that comes their way with zeal and energy, even tasks that are useless or wrong. They are too stupid to discriminate between important tasks and trivia. They will be bound by procedure and correct form rather that output. They take pride in doing things the hard way and fail to realise when to give up. Organisations need these people like salmonella in the Christmas turkey.

Two options are available to those who have simple and hardworking subordinates: sack them or side-load them to posts where they can inflict minimum damage. In modern organisations managers in this category will fall for the allure of Just in Time, BS5750 or Total Quality Management, not to mention Office Procedure on the Use and Disposal of Lavatory Paper. In the zest for hard work, these people are so obsessed by methodology that they lose sight of the need for an end-product.

Shrewd and lazy. These people have lots of ideas, but are only galvanised into action if it is absolutely necessary. They will find the quickest way of doing things, disregard form and concentrate on outcome. By delegating tasks, they will allocate time to think and plan. The shrewd and lazy manager also gets on well with others in the organisation because he realises he needs their help to get things done. According to Clausewitz, of the four types, he is the most valuable to organisations.

Clausewitz's model remains applicable to organisations today. Consider some of the benefits the shrewd and lazy manager can bring to the organisation:

- As he is lazy he will not get involved in traditional ways of working if they are time-consuming. Instead he will find new techniques to get the job done.
- He will find the most convenient way of achieving this.

- He will delegate downwards where jobs can be performed by cheaper labour.
- He will challenge traditional ways of doing things and keep the organisation dynamic. As a consequence he may well discover new markets, technologies, products and services.
- He will cultivate good relations with colleagues because he needs other people to get things done.
- He will use technology to save time.

Winning the organisation game is about overcoming the barriers, human and organisational, to gaining power in the organisation with the minimum of effort and maximum rewards. It is about finding the quickest and easiest way of avoiding or removing the obstacles to power. It is about maximising the returns and minimising the effort.

Let's be clear about what I mean by power. While this word can be used to describe wealth, status and influence, it can also mean an individual's ability to maintain control over his activities with the minimum of interference from others. Power in the organisation is about deciding what you want and making sure that you get it.

Consider the following example and see how everyone has access to the type of power that suits his or her needs.

Old Archie's brewery is a small family-run business, with aunts, uncles and cousins holding senior posts. Following the death of his grandfather, David has inherited the business and has taken over the role of managing director. Alarmed at the company's poor performance, he is investigating how it might be improved. As it is a family business he feels unable to sack any of the staff. He therefore uses Clausewitz's model as the basis for the changes he makes.

Aunt Jess is the company accountant (book-keeper) known for her kindly manner and old-fashioned ways. When David suggests introducing some more up-to-date accounting systems he is told, 'Laddie, I've been doing my books with carbon paper, biro pen and ledger book since 1940 and I'm no' about to change to a fancy computer! Ye'll have me flyin' to the moon next!' David places her in the category of *simple and hardworking* and decides to give her the new post of 'Tour Guide for Old Archie's Visitor Centre'. Aunt Jess is delighted with her new role as she sees herself as the keeper of traditional values in the company.

Uncle Bert is the chief brewer. He is renowned in the trade for his love of the product and little else. Although Old Archie's brew is a high-quality beer, Uncle Bert has made no attempt to diversify into other types and the competition has consequently filled the gaps. Uncle Bert falls into the category of *simple and lazy*. David decides to appoint Cousin Jamie to the post of Product Development Manager. Jamie has recently graduated from a top business school with an MBA and is regarded as a bit of a high flyer. He is appointed on the grounds that he is *shrewd, hardworking* and is likely to make sure that Uncle Bert does as he is told. Uncle Bert is happy with this arrangement as he can follow the instructions of Cousin Jamie and avoid the responsibility of launching major initiatives of his own, while Cousin Jamie has the power to flex his managerial muscles.

Cousin Emma is a freelance accountant who has been involved in a number of highly successful business start-up ventures. David invites her to join the company to take over Aunt Jess's 'accountancy' function and to act as his right-hand woman. Emma is *shrewd and hard-working* and is delighted to have the opportunity to practise her accountancy skills and tackle a number of interesting challenges in a familiar and protected environment.

David, who is *shrewd and lazy*, has delegated downwards to Emma and Jamie on the grounds that they can be relied upon to ensure the smooth day-to-day running of Old Archie's. In the meantime, he himself will concentrate on preparing a strategic plan to drive the company forward.

Personal Experience Exercise
$ Can you identify a manager in your organisation who has become embittered by the way he has been treated? Does the title LOSER fit?

$ Can you also see a manager who has done well out of the system? Does the title WINNER describe him?

$ How far could you openly admit that you really do not give a damn for your organisation and are out to gain power for yourself — EASILY/WITH DIFFICULTY/NOT AT ALL?

$ Think of the training courses you have attended. How often have the instructors included material that might help you gain power at the expense of the party line of your organisation?

THE NEED FOR PARANOIA

The conventional view of organisations, as teams which work together for a common and higher good, is a myth. Organisations, and those who work in them, are out to stop you from winning, each in his own special way and each for his own special reasons. It will be obvious, therefore, that one of the first things the winning manager must do is adopt a cynical and paranoic approach to organisational life. Expect the system to be against you and planning your downfall now, and you will not be disappointed later. Expect even the seemingly inanimate fabric of the organisation to be your enemy and your vigilance will be rewarded.

Look at the following map of yourself in relation to others in your management environment. It will underline the need for you to mistrust everyone in the organisational structure. It is a 'management cross', with you crucified at its centre. Your superiors and subordinates stand above and beneath you. Your peers and your fellow organisation members lurk on either side. Think how each group, from its own special perspective, has interests and needs that are at odds with your aim of achieving power. Think how, without their being conscious of it, their very existence means that they must act against your interests in the pursuit of rewards in organisational life. Let us look at them one by one.

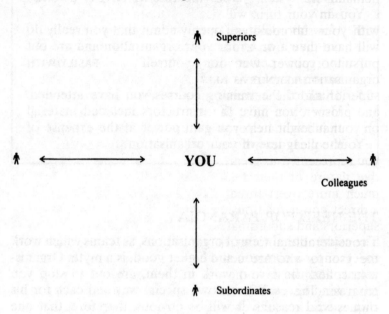

The Management Cross

Superiors

YOU

Colleagues

Subordinates

From above, you will be subjected to pressure from the weight of the organisation. This will force you to channel all your energies to achieve the goals of the organisation rather than your own winning manager's agenda, the aim of gaining power. There is no malice here. The organisation has the morally neutral motivation of the rattle-snake which bites you, not because it is malevolent, but because that is what rattle-snakes do. Organisations undermine their managers because that is what organisations do.

Pressure from above, however, will not all be impersonal. Your superiors will translate the dictates and needs of the organisation into their own ways of extracting effort and action from you. Moreover, each layer of senior management will apply its own pressure, according to a peculiar mixture of personal whim and organisational opportunism. Expect the people above you to screw you. Their self-interest demands it. Their very survival as senior managers demands it.

You, in your turn, will need to adopt a similar approach with your subordinates. This will be far from easy as they will have their own agendas which will be inimical to your pursuit of power. One of the toughest problems for the organisation member is to be caught between the will of a superior and the intransigence of subordinates. To survive and prosper, you must develop ways of imposing your will on your subordinates or you will join the ranks of the losers.

Your colleagues who are of equal rank and standing to you represent your greatest obstacle. Although the competitive nature of their relationship with you makes them a much more overt threat to your survival, you are not in a direct power relationship with them as you are with your superiors and subordinates. Dealing with them will demand a considerable amount of applied skill and energy. Of all the groups who are set against you in the organisation, your colleagues have the greatest investment in halting your progress. They will certainly include individuals or even cliques who are actively seeking your downfall.

Talk of the need for paranoia may seem far-fetched. I hope it is in your case. But long years of organisational life, watching managers exploit and be exploited, tell me that it is the normal state of affairs. The price of gaining power over these forces is, at the very least, the need to be permanently on one's guard against the machinations of others. Organisations and the people in them will keep you down if you do not take active steps to beat them.

Having started this book on a promissory note it would appear that we have drifted pretty quickly into a pessimistic tone—not so. You must be fully aware of the hostilities in your managerial environment; but you can also be reassured by their existence. Your opposition comes from other human beings with their all-too human characteristics and frailties. Acknowledge this and you are one step ahead of them. Your opponents will be acting unconsciously. Unlike you, they will not be working to a carefully conceived and orchestrated plan based upon a sound knowledge of human weaknesses and susceptibilities. Once you know where your enemies lie, and have realised your will to beat them, you have only to use the weapons that will defeat them. In the rest of this book I will show you:

- How to identify pointless rules.
- How to identify people who will prevent you from winning.
- How to be more cautious about the influence of groups.
- How to set and attain goals.
- How to understand the power structure of the organisation and your route through it.
- How to obtain the compliance of others.
- How to ditch losers' ideas.
- How to develop a winning management style.

People are central to the organisation game and will be instrumental in helping you to achieve power. First, however, you must learn how to use and manipulate them.

Personal Experience Exercise

$ Put names to the management cross, as it affects you. Identify your immediate superiors. Name the group that is subordinate to you. Look either side of you and work out those who are on the same organisational level as you.

$ Ask yourself, 'When did I last feel "used" by my organisation?'

$ When did you last see a fellow manager abused by the system?

$ Have you ever felt the pressure of being caught between the requirements of senior management and the intransigence of your subordinates?

$ Can you think of an occasion when your colleagues, your immediate peers on the management cross, might have threatened your pursuit of power?

$ Look about you. Take each of the arms of your management cross and think of someone on that arm who made a gross miscalculation by not realis-

> ing the threat to his position from the people
> around him.

THE EFFORT BARGAIN

'Slavery they can have anywhere. It is a weed that grows in
every soil,' said Edmund Burke in his speech on conciliation
with America in 1775. For 'slavery' read 'organisation'. The
propagandists will, of course, ridicule this idea. But let us
analyse one of the favourite tools for inducing the manager
to work even harder: the effort bargain.

This is the theoretical bargain that an individual strikes
with the organisation. It relates to the amount of effort and
energy that you are expected to put into a job, and the
rewards, both material and non-material,[6] that you receive
in return. Theorists write of the effort bargain as though
there existed some form of equity between two contracting
partners. Your own experience will tell you, however, that
the organisation's expectations of managers' efforts are
infinite. How many of you, for example, have quite happily
signed employment contracts where the job description con-
tained that innocuous-looking phrase 'and other duties as
required'? On the other hand, the benefits accruing to you
are strictly circumscribed. Quite simply, organisations are
out to extract as much effort as they can from you in return
for as little as possible.

The expectation that you will give your very best to the
organisation conflicts with your natural instinct to gain
power for yourself. From your side, the bargain is an imposition that controls your life. You agree to it so that you can
live in a certain style and with a certain status. Yet to the
frustration of the self-centred 'inner you'—that part of your
psyche that has the job of looking after your best interests[7]—
this will always represent too little, too late, for too much
effort. The effort bargain is inherently staked against your
needs. While you must pay lip-service to it, such a one-
sided bargain can clearly have no claim on your loyalty. You

should see the effort bargain for what it is—a device used by the organisation to hold you back from your natural drives to gain power for your own ends.

Winning, however, is about more than merely rejecting the unequal content of the effort bargain. The price of failure in the organisation game is losing it, and losers not only fail to attain power for themselves, they spend the rest of their careers concentrating on all those activities which are typically associated with losers. Here are just a few examples:

- Attending meetings where there is no political decision to be made.
- Caring about the task, the organisation and its people.
- Treating existing rules with sanctity rather than contempt.
- Doing a task that could have been delegated.
- Performing a task to a higher standard than is necessary.
- Performing a task for which the team gets the credit.
- Being available and allowing others to interrupt you.
- Volunteering.
- Reading every memo, letter, report and other type of document which lands in your in-tray.
- Refusing to say 'no' when asked to do something.
- Asking for permission to do something.

The worst aspect of being a loser is having your life defined and controlled by external events over which you have little or no control. You discover that you are no longer an acting agent in the ordering of your own world. In short, you win the organisation game or you go under.

All this may sound very daunting. The fact that you are reading this book, however, should be a major source of encouragement. You have obviously acknowledged that you are a potential winner: all you now have to do is make it happen. Understand from the outset that you have a choice and that you are capable of winning, *provided your desire is strong enough*, but you must be prepared to make the necessary effort and sacrifices or you will end up as a loser.

A major theme of this book is the need for the winning manager to ditch those ways of thought that are inimical to winning. You will be shown how to adopt the right mental attitude, and one of the early lessons in this process is to realise that you must be single-minded in pursuing your will to gain power. You must get what you want to get out of the organisation, not what your superiors, your subordinates and certainly not your colleagues think you deserve. None of this has anything to do with the notion of deserving: it is about learning that you do not get out of the system what you put in. There is a lot more in terms of power—in terms of control over your life—to be squeezed out of it than it would have you think.

Winning managers realise this and act accordingly. They know they must always be on the look-out for opportunities to achieve power and that this requires a winner's state of mind. Losers allow themselves to become the creatures of the organisation and its members. They are content to put the needs and goals of the organisation before their own.

If you want to win, you have to free yourself from the rules, made by others, which are designed to bind you to what the organisation wants you to do rather than what will be right for you.[8] As you will see, the barriers to your achievement are largely illusory: they will crumble if you refuse to acknowledge them.

As I have said earlier, to be a winner in the organisation game you must add to your paranoia a strong dose of psychopathy, the character trait that allows you to concentrate on dominating the managerial environment.[9] Above all, you require the will to overcome the inhibitions that have been learnt as part of the process of 'civilisation'.[10] You must recognise that there are no rules other than those you make for yourself. Once this step has been taken, there is nothing but your inner self to stand between you and winning.

Personal Experience Exercise

$ Have you ever felt that your good will is exploited by an ever-demanding senior management?

$ Have you ever felt that the organisation makes unreasonable demands on you, but that you have to comply or lose out?

$ Can you identify someone in your organisation who seems to get on, without deserving to?

$ Is there a manager among your colleagues who works his arse off but never seems to be appreciated for the effort?

$ Think of an occasion when you have thought to yourself, 'The rules of this organisation are crooked.'

CONVENTIONAL MORALITY

In your pursuit of power, most of the teachings of conventional morality will be useless. You will find terms such as 'loyalty', 'discipline', 'subordination of individual interest to the general interest'.[11] Most of the textbooks, in fact, would have one believe that managers are no different from Franciscan friars. At worst, organisational philosophy is a losers' charter which justifies the actions of those who are too weak or too servile to stand above the herd and take on the challenge of winning. Conventional morality, backed by conventional philosophy, assumes that individuals are happy to bow to such notions as service, loyalty, ethics, and caring about the organisation and its interests. To do so, however, is a sure recipe for being dragged into a set of losing strategies.

As a winner you need to see that morality is a subjective idea. There is no such thing as a moral or immoral act, only an act that is interpreted as moral or immoral by others.[12] If you can learn the art of rejecting the judgements that others may make of your behaviour and stand above them, then you are free to create your own morality. This is not as outrageous as it may appear. Morality in organisational behaviour is always a matter of personal choice. Unfortunately, however, the conventional approach is endorsed by those who have a loser's mentality and is heavily biased against you. It is always coloured by others' self-interest and by the debilitating need of others to 'feel good'. What you need to ask is, 'What are the vested interests of those who judge action as moral or immoral?' For the winning manager, the judgement of all members of the organisation is suspect. They are all out to get you, by enslaving you in their ways of looking at the world.

This is not to say that winning managers should act as if they were entirely independent of others and of the morality of others. Remember the Winner's Commandments: take note of the realities of organisational life and appear to conform to them. What separates you from the losers is how far you allow the dictates of conventional morality to deflect you from the pursuit of power for yourself. All your actions must be subordinated to the higher aim of personal power. The end justifies the means.

The true mark of the winning manager is a determination to get your way despite all the obstacles. Losers do not have this determination and so decline into the role of subservience to the organisation, to its people or to their perception of a 'correct' way of behaving, coming to believe that this has some sort of universal moral validity.

Charles Perrow describes professionals—managers who are trained for a specific set of roles in organisations—as the 'ultimate eunuchs'.[13] They are so indoctrinated by the organisation that they are incapable of acting and thinking for themselves. Winning the organisation game is only possible if you take the positive step to liberate yourself from this 'slave mentality' and realise that there is no 'should be', only what you want there to be.

Personal Experience Exercise

$ Ask yourself, 'How far would my superiors back me if I made a major mistake that jeopardised them or the organisation?'

$ Can you identify a manager around you who seems to have taken the organisation's ways of doing things totally on board?

CONVENTIONAL WISDOM

The would-be winning manager needs to be very suspicious of what passes for conventional wisdom, as it is applied to managerial life. The organisation is full of old-timers, managers who see it as their duty to guide their juniors into the ways of the company. Such juniors may be senior to them in the hierarchy, but they still use the pressure of their time-based seniority to try to bring the newcomer into what they see as the right ways, the ways that 'we do things around here'.[14] Winners beware!

These people have the power of common sense on their side. Yet common sense is far from common, least of all amongst those who have spent years in the system, learning its way of doing business and perhaps receiving partial reward for their loyalty and compliance. As a winning manager you must cultivate the art of challenge, albeit silent, to everything that the organisation requires of you. Old-timers, who have been thoroughly indoctrinated in losers' ways, are not the people to guide you on to a winning track. You need to be aware of some of the 'common-sense' notions that they will try to impose on you, for you are going to have to rid yourself of them and many others besides. Here are some of the major organisational lies that will be fed to you.

Hard work is the way to achieve reward
This idea has a long history. In Western culture, one strain of it may be traced to the so-called 'Protestant work ethic'.[15] This no longer has anything to do with religion and has taken on an insidious life of its own. It has led to the widespread acceptance that there is something inherently deserving in effort for its own sake, a notion that is deadly to the winner. If you listen to it you will face two dangerous consequences.

First, you will fall into the trap of believing that hard work is an end in itself. All around you there are managers beavering away, yet achieving nothing. For them, being busy is important; it allows them to feel that they are playing their part and being good organisational members. Watch them arrive at 8 a.m. every morning, scurrying around with clip-boards and wearing a permanent expression of agitation for no apparent purpose. See the look on their faces when their undirected efforts do not produce results. They have clearly not considered what Frederick Taylor[16] referred to as the need to work 'smarter not harder'. A typical loser behaves as though winning comes from the effort put into organisational life, as though pure effort alone is worthy of eventual reward.

The second and perhaps more alarming aspect of this obsession is the belief that achievement of results is less important than the applied effort. The winner in the organisation game is the one who can achieve results with minimum effort. The loser feels that achievement without effort is somehow less worthy than the expenditure of sweat, blood and tears.

You must be loyal to the organisation and its members

This is a foolish notion that the would-be winning manager should dismiss instantly. What did loyalty achieve for the thousands who worked for organisations, only to be made redundant overnight? Organisations are out to exploit their employees. Realise this and defend your own interests. Your *seeming* loyalty may be bought for the time being, but you must always remember that you owe nothing to anybody, least of all to the organisation or its members.

A job worth doing is worth doing well

This is one of the most serious obstacles in your path. Just as some losers are obsessed with hard work for its own sake, so others are mesmerised by the pursuit of excellence. All activities, no matter how trivial, must be channelled towards excellence. The winning manager needs to learn that 'the best is the enemy of the good'.[17] Once the job in hand is completed to the required minimum standard, sit back, pour yourself a malt whisky and watch your colleagues run around like a pack of lemmings. Doing things to a standard that is higher than absolutely necessary is a waste of valuable time and energy.

Of course, fallacies such as these run deep in the culture of organisational life. As a winner you must not challenge them openly—indeed, you will find it useful to champion them in public. Keep in mind the seventh Winner's Commandment: *Say one thing and do another.*

Personal Experience Exercise

$ Think of an example of a manager who has achieved success with minimum effort.

$ Now think of an example of the opposite: a manager who has put into the organisation a lot of effort, but who has reaped little or no reward.

$ Can you identify a manager in your company who takes a pride in striving to do things thoroughly and well, even when they are unimportant?

WINNER'S WAYS

Being a winner in the organisation game is not an easy option: the game itself is played under adverse conditions. For a start, it is like blind man's buff, so that you are unaware of your enemies' activities. This is both a weakness and a strength. You may not be clear about the shaping of events around you, but neither are your opponents. Your strength is that you realise this and can manipulate accordingly the information available to your opponents. You know that you are blindfolded and can take steps to discover more about the environment, at the same time making it more difficult for the opposition to know what you yourself are engaged in. You also have the added advantage of knowing that your opponents are unaware that they are playing a game. Your colleagues consider that the organisation, as a harmless entity, requires no analysis, no thought, no strategy. Most of them have already set themselves up to lose.

Being a winning manager requires strength and determination. Above all it takes guts to reject a life-time of false philosophy and acknowledge that you are on your own. You may have allies and helpers, but their loyalty, however much they may protest otherwise, is to themselves, just as yours must be to yourself. It takes the guts to realise that parts of the inner you are only too ready to play the game according to your opponents' rules;[18] that you must discipline and train your inner self to play the game wholeheartedly, for you and for your ends alone. Lastly, it takes guts to realise that you *can* achieve power over your life in the organisation and become a winner.

2 The Enemy Within

As a winning manager you must confront internal as well as external enemies who are determined to thwart you. In order to stand apart from and above the drives that make lesser mortals behave as they do, you need to know about the human psyche and the driving forces that lie between individuals and their actions. Once you can recognise these forces in others you will see them for what they are, the mere products of human frailty, but you also need to see them in yourself if you are to subordinate them to your aim of winning the organisation game.

In this chapter I want to introduce you to the vocabulary of Sigmund Freud and some of his later followers. In particular, I want to show you how one approach to Freud's psychology has led to a useful understanding of two important, related problems: why so many managers know what they should do to achieve the required result but do something else entirely, and why so many of them know what could be done, but do anything but what is required to be the winner. Look at the two diagrams opposite. In each case something is dragging the manager away from the achievement of, on the one hand winner's goals and, on the other, the best possible outcome.

What force or set of forces seems intent on preventing talented and intelligent managers from fulfilling their potential and achieving their goals? Sigmund Freud's famous Triad of Id, Ego and Super Ego will help to provide the answer, enabling you to understand what is going on, deep in individuals' psyches, and also to understand the psychology of losers in the organisation.

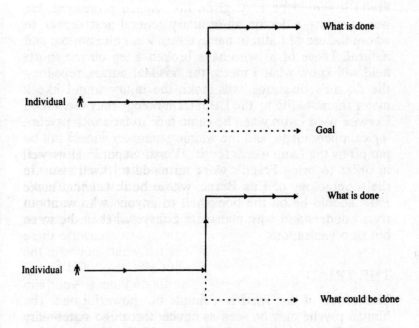

Personal Experience Exercise

$ Can you identify someone in your organisation who consistently fails to achieve what you know he could achieve?

$ Can you think of two occasions when you have set yourself goals and failed to achieve them because of your own fault?

$ Ask yourself when you last felt that you were not achieving in your organisation what you know you could achieve.

For many, talk of 'ids' and 'egos' is intimidating. Like all technical jargon, these words are a threat to the ignorance of the outsider. You, however, must be prepared to look beyond such short-sighted prejudices, and in the case of

Freud it should be easy, given his original profession. He was of course a doctor, an ordinary general practitioner, to whom the use of Latin to name things was quite normal and natural. Those of us who have broken a leg on the sports field will know what I mean: the hospital nurses, repeating the doctor's diagnosis, will make the injury sound like a major threat to life by the Latin terminology they use. Freud likewise used Latin when he came face to face with psychological phenomena, and the winning manager should not be put off by the Latin words for 'it', 'I' and 'Super I'. However, in order to bring Freud's work up to date I shall also use the terminology of Eric Berne, whose book *Games People Play*[1] should be on the bookshelf of anyone who wants to try to understand why managers behave as they do, in or out of organisations.

THE TRIAD

The notion of the Triad is a simple but powerful one. The human psyche may be seen as having three ego states—the Id, the Ego and the Super Ego—each of which builds up psychological energy and forces the individual to behave in one of three generalised ways. Norman Dixon[2] shows that these ego states are more than just an abstract idea. Modern experiments have revealed that different parts of the brain control the behaviours associated with them and that typical ego state behaviour can be induced or suppressed by physical intervention in particular parts of the brain.

Although each ego state governs a general type of behaviour, the behaviour of the individual human being is a product of his or her own experience. People have their own, albeit unconscious, preferences for particular ways of discharging energy from the three ego states and their behaviour patterns are also affected by the balance of power that exists between the ego states.

Let's start by looking at the Id, the fundamental building block of the human psyche. The human organism needs to survive in what is, right from the start, a hostile environment. Chance alone will not guarantee its survival: some inner

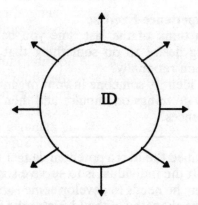

mechanism is needed, which seeks to impose the tiny will on the environment. This is the job of the Id. Eric Berne renamed this the 'Child', for he saw it as being the earliest stage of development of the Triad, already in place in the psyche of the newborn infant. The Id contains the natural drives that push the individual towards behaviour that will ensure its survival. In young children it contains the imperatives of 'I want' and 'feed me'; in later life it is characterised by will-power and determination to get one's way. In describing the general characteristics of the Id to my students, I draw their attention to my terrier bitch who is a living embodiment of the concept of the Id. She appears to have a checklist of Id-based behaviours that she employs when meeting a new phenomenon—'Can I eat it?' 'Can I sexually assault it?' 'If neither of these is possible, I shall fight it!'

In human beings the Id is also consciousness and the source of spontaneity, of love of life and of creativity. Above all, it is the source of will. The unrestrained Id will seek to dominate its environment and to remove obstacles that stand in its way. It is selfish, thinking only of the needs of ME, and leaves the job of worrying about the consequences of behaviour to other parts of the Triad. It is psychopathic in its disregard for the wants and needs of others. Without the Id the individual could not survive.

Personal Experience Exercise
$ Can you think of the last time you had an over-
    whelming desire to do something that you could
    not explain rationally?
$ Can you identify someone in your organisation who
    seems to do things on impulse and then regrets the
    consequences?

When unrestrained the Id is a potential danger to the personality it serves. If the individual is to survive strangulation by
those about him, he needs to develop some form of check on
the would-be psychopathy of the Id. Enter the Super Ego.

The duty of this member of the Triad is to channel the
drives of the Id into behaviour that is conducive to prosper-
ing in the environment in which the individual must live.

From our first moments of life the Super Ego begins its
task of learning the rules of survival. These are largely social,
and the role of parents in teaching them is underlined by
Berne's translation of 'Super Ego' as 'Parent'. The Super
Ego is very adept at learning what social psychologists call
'socialisation': it is constantly on the look-out for the rules
that will ensure its survival. Every time the behaviour of the
unrestrained Id is checked, the Super Ego converts these
setbacks into generalised rules about the way the world
works; later these will be translated into language—'I must'
or 'I must not'. But the process precedes language and
rational thought. It is unconscious and even in later years,
when the Super Ego is still going about its task of internalis-
ing the rules of socialisation, it is, to use the language of
information technology, transparent to the user. The Super
Ego's influence will appear as the manifestations of what we
refer to as the conscience. It's prime function is to direct our
behaviour to keep it within the bounds of our social group.

Over time, a process of generalisation and externalisation
takes place. 'I must' and 'I must not' are extended to include
others in the environment—'you must' and 'you must not'.
Those readers who are well acquainted with children will be
familiar with the process whereby a pile of teddy bears and

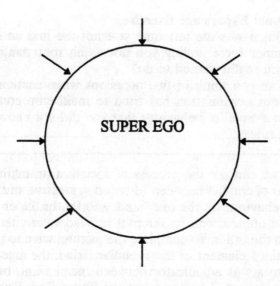

dolls receives a rebuke for the untidiness of the play-room:
'Mummy will be very cross with you if you don't put your
toys away!' My terrier recently received a finger-wagging
ticking-off from a three-year-old whose Super Ego was anxious to share its recently learnt rule that 'You mustn't wee-
wee in the street, the neighbours don't like it'.

Norman Dixon, in his fascinating book on the psychology
of misused power, *Our Own Worst Enemy*, sums up the
necessity for this Super Ego learning process.[3] In his view
three survival functions derive from it. First, there is the
need for human beings to cooperate. We are, after all, pack
animals and most of our endeavours require the subordination of the individual will to common and cooperative
goals. Second, the complexity of human society requires
obedience to increasingly complex sets of rules merely to
survive. Lastly, he cites the need for the individual to draw
upon the good will of others. Man, the pack animal, needs
the support of the pack.[4] None of these functions would
be taken care of by the unrestrained Id, out only for the
gratification of its owner's inner will.

Personal Experience Exercise
$ When was the last time you felt the grip of some
'inner force' telling you not to do something that
you really wanted to do?
$ Can you think of two occasions when someone in
your organisation has tried to make you conform
to a 'rule' of behaviour that you did not know was
a rule?

So far we can see the process of socialisation taking place
in terms of conflict between Id-based aggressive and dominating behaviour on the one hand, and the brake on this by
the environment and its internal representative, the Super
Ego, on the other. To complete the picture, we need to look
at the third element of the Freudian Triad, the Ego, whose
job is to act as adjudicator between the 'I want' of the Id
and the 'I must, I must not' of the Super Ego. Eric Berne
calls it the 'Adult' because its emergence marks the growth
of the incipient human being. As we develop, so our behaviour
is characterised by rational, logical and objective evaluation
and decision-making. For Eric Berne,[5] the Ego is primarily
concerned with processing data; Norman Dixon,[6] however,
reminds us of its selfish pragmatism. He notes that the Ego
takes account only of the physical constraints of the environment and the dictates of input of the Super Ego. Beyond that,
it is content to allow the Id to get away with what it can.

Donald Bannister drew a graphic image of the workings
of the Triad. He described the relationship between Id,
Super Ego and Ego[7] as a battle for control of an individual's
behaviour conducted in a dark cellar, between a wellbred
Victorian spinster and a sex-crazed monkey, adjudicated
over by a rather diffident bank clerk. A less graphic
illustration of their relationship might be seen as shown in
the figure opposite.

Let us look at some of the types of behaviour that are
governed by the three ego states. The list opposite is not
exhaustive and is intended merely to give a general feel of
the style of each ego state's influence.

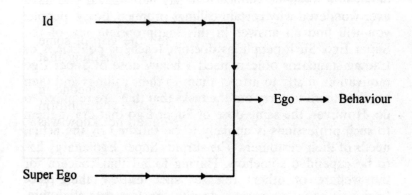

Id

Ego → Behaviour

Super Ego

TYPICAL EGO STATE BEHAVIOUR

	Positive	*Negative*
ID	Creative	Destructive
	Spontaneous	Impetuous
	Humorous	Wishful
	Active	thinking
	Erotic	Sulking
		Lewd
EGO		Deciding
		Evaluating
		Planning
SUPER EGO	Directing	Inhibiting
	Guiding	Prohibiting
	Protecting	Punishing
	Caring	Judging
	Nurturing	Stifling

In the case of the Super Ego and Id I have distinguished between the positive and the negative aspects of behaviour induced by them. The positive aspects speak for themselves; the negative aspects come from the inappropriate use of their positive counterparts. We shall look at these in more detail in a moment. Suffice it to say here that if you have ever wondered why certain callings produce 'bossy' people, you will find an answer in this inappropriate use of the Super Ego. Such people as doctors, teachers, politicians or trading standards officers need a heavy dose of Super Ego motivation, firstly to attract them to their callings and then to allow them to carry out the tasks that they are required to do. However, the same dose of Super Ego that draws them to such professions is unlikely to be satisfied by the actual needs of their customers. The surplus Super Ego energy has to be expended somehow. Having found that concern for the welfare of others releases such energy, these professionals carry on caring, despite the fact that their customers resent their concern.

Personal Experience Exercise

$ Look at each of the types of behaviour listed on page 29. Think of occasions when you last found yourself using each of them.

$ Think of a time when you may have used each of them 'inappropriately'—when some other type of behaviour might have been more useful.

$ Can you think of examples of another manager in your organisation using the negative behaviours 'inappropriately'?

Behaviour from each of the ego states is normal and natural, recognisable in ourselves and others about us. It results from a build-up of something resembling static in a particular area of the brain, followed by a release of the accumulated energy through the vehicle of behaviour. The form that behaviour takes will relate to past experiences.[8] Suppose, for example, that past experience has taught the Ego that creativity is a very effective way of dealing with the demands of the Id, notwithstanding the dictates of, first, the Super Ego, and second, the environment. If these creative drives are consistently thwarted, the ego state energy still has to be released in some way. Since creativity has proved unproductive, the Id will seek another channel for its frustrated demands. Unfortunately, in most aspects of human interaction, and most of all in the highly restricting context of managerial life, negative or even destructive behaviour is less easily thwarted. The destruction of the creativity of others, the private pleasures of *Schadenfreude*[9] or a retreat into sullen cantankerousness are all too available to the thwarted Id as a means of releasing energy, and you can probably think of several people in your organisation who demonstrate this type of behaviour with predictable regularity.

EGO STATE BALANCE

From this account of the workings of the Triad it might seem that each part takes an equal role in determining human behaviour. The Id provides for the survival of the individual by trying to dominate the environment, the Super Ego provides the necessary checking influences and the Ego, with its rationality, merely steers a middle course. An idealised view of the human psyche might therefore see the balance between the influences of the various ego states as being something like this:

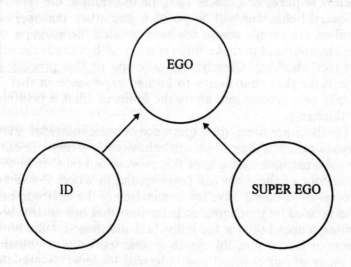

Here, the rational, evaluating Ego has a firm grip on the influences over behaviour of the subordinate Id and Super Ego. Behaviour will be governed by rationality, albeit a rationality that is driven by the other two ego states and the Ego's tendency to go for the option of 'What it can get away with'.

However, as Norman Dixon argues,[10] life is not like that. Although the majority of us occupy some middle ground of relative socialisation, some are only socialised to a superficial level and others are oversocialised, being governed by the dictates of the internalised rules of their Super Egos. Looked at schematically we might see the possibilities as follows.

In some of us the Id, despite the efforts of the environment and the Super Ego working on its behalf, remains dominant in the struggle for control (see figure opposite). Here the will to dominate the environment is stronger than the forces speaking out on behalf of socialisation and conformity. Even the rational, moderating influences of the Ego are subject to the imperatives of the stronger Id. At times, individuals like this will be driven to behaviour that satisfies the needs of the Id, even though it may not conform to what society requires or expects. In some individuals, the type of Id-based behaviour will be positive: the artist, the original thinker, are people whose Ids have resisted the attempts of the environment to make them comply with convention and 'correct' thinking. Clearly, the outcome of this process is behaviour that contributes to human experience in that it breaks new ground and alters the limits of what is possible or thinkable.

On the other hand, the experience of some individual may have channelled their Id-driven behaviour into negative outlets. An extreme example of this process can be seen in the behaviour of those we call psychopaths, in whom the same process of Id-based drive for domination of the environment is expressed by psychopathic behaviour that has destructive consequences, both for the individual and those around him. Norman Dixon sees this psychopathic tendency as present in many of our political and industrial leaders.[11] A notable

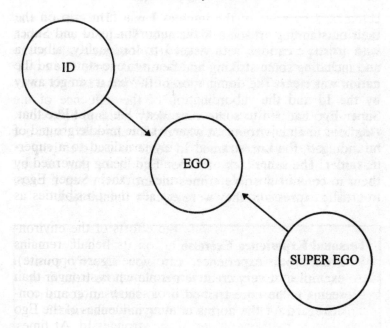

example in recent British history was the late Robert Maxwell whose will to dominate the environment of commerce seemed to be little restrained by his Super Ego.

The degree of freedom allowed to the Id will differ according to the relative strengths of the accompanying Ego and Super Ego. The stronger the dominance of the Id, however, the greater the likelihood of the individual's behaviour being outrageous in one form or another. For me, one of the most telling pieces of evidence for the accuracy of Freud's analysis became apparent when I was observing the behaviour of criminal psychopaths – or at least, those who had been identified as such by their crimes. I was visiting the hospital for the criminally insane at Broadmoor in Hampshire, sandwiched between the Royal Military Academy Sandhurst and the famous English public school that produces military 'toughs', Wellington. Two things amazed me. The first was the horrific crimes that had been committed by most of the inmates I met. The second was their outstanding artistic achievement. The place was awash with artistic creations, with visual arts dominating the scene and including some striking and beautiful work. The explanation was clear. The domination of the inmates' ego states by the Id and the subordination of the influence of the Super Ego had led to some very nasty criminal behaviour. Confined in an environment where this behaviour could not be indulged, the unrestrained Id came to use creativity as its outlet. The same lack of Super Ego brake that allowed them to commit horrible crimes meant that, when it came to artistic expression, they were equally uninhibited.

Personal Experience Exercise
$ From your experience, can you identify some examples of very creative people whose behaviour seems to be unrestrained or to show an eccentric disregard for the norms of everyday behaviour?

At the other end of the socialisation process we find the'oversocialised' individual. Here the behaviour of the individual is governed heavily by the Super Ego and what that ego state has learnt in terms of the 'rules' of conduct for living (see figure opposite). Individuals who share this pattern have difficulty in overcoming the dictates of their overactive Super Ego. They will tend to see life as governed by rules that, by the process of internalisation, may be elevated to the status of moral precepts. Such unfortunates may be so oppressed by their Super Ego's urge to dominate the Triad that in managerial life they are driven by the desire to continue traditional ways of doing the business of the organisation rather than innovate. The biggest danger for them and those about them is that their Super Ego will tend to emphasise conformity at the expense of effectiveness. They will diligently look for rules to govern their behaviour before acting. For them, management will be more 'an art form' than a means of achieving ends.

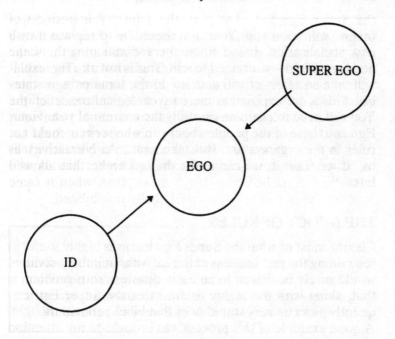

Personal Experience Exercise

$ Can you spot someone you know whose behaviour
  seems to be governed by 'the rules' of your organisation?

$ Can you think of an occasion when you were reluc-
  tant to do something because it conflicted with the
  'way things are normally done'?

The purpose of this book is to help you become a winning
manager by overcoming the constraints that stand between
you and winning. One of the major inhibiting factors is the
restriction of your Id, with its potential to drive you to win,
by the dampening and debilitating influence of the Super
Ego. If you are to triumph in the organisation game this
enemy within must be conquered. My method is to expose

the Super Ego for what it is, the arbitrary imposition of others' will upon you. Your aim should be to replace it by a new socialisation, based upon the rational pursuit of the needs of the Id—your need to win. This is not an easy task. It will take an effort of will and, no doubt, some pain, as cherished ideas are exposed as mere psychological constructions. You will need to examine carefully the content of your Super Ego and those of the people about you who seem to make the rules in the organisation. But take heart. As Nietzsche tells us, 'if we train it, we can make the conscience kiss us as it bites'.[12]

THE IDIOCY OF RULES

Clearly, most of what the Super Ego learns is highly useful in restraining the recklessness of the Id; without it the individual would surely be driven to an early disaster. Your problem is that, along with the highly useful rules, the Super Ego frequently picks up very stupid ones that block rational thought. A good example of this process was brought to my attention by a friend of mine, with whom I was recently walking on a flagged pavement. In the middle of a perfectly rational conversation, he began to upbraid me in quite a judgemental tone. Surely I knew that one was not supposed to tread on the cracks? I, of course, knew no such thing, although as a child I had played the game that the 'bears would get me' if I trod on the pavement cracks. To my colleague, however, avoiding the cracks had become a serious Super Ego imperative that, for him, was a universally accepted rule. He obviously expended a great deal of time and thought on adjusting his stride to avoid treading on cracks between flagstones, sometimes taking unnaturally long strides and at others being reduced to wasteful 'fairy steps', rather than merely using the path in front of him to reach his destination. I suspect the same Super Ego process hindered his process through managerial life, where he was constrained by all sorts of spurious rules about how one should go about doing things, rather than concentrating upon effective ways of achieving the desired outcome.

The problem with such rule-learning behaviour is that we

are all subject to it. Let me invite you to take part in a practical exercise that will make the point. Join the dots of the two diagrams below, without taking your pen off the paper, using only three straight lines for the first diagram and only four for the second:

Without very much difficulty you will produce an answer that looks like this:

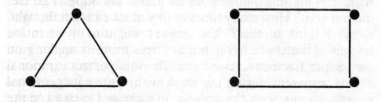

Now try this exercise. Join the dots in the next diagram, without taking your pen off the paper, using only four straight lines:

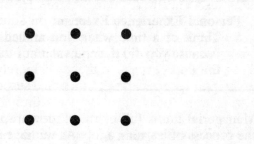

Spend three minutes trying this exercise. The answer is on page 43.

You have been set up. I have colluded with your Super Ego to ensure that, for most of you, this will be a difficult if not impossible task. It has nothing to do with intelligence. I regularly watch highly intelligent people fail to accomplish what is essentially a simple manoeuvre. However, your Super Ego will have taken the rules of the first two exercises and imputed from them a rule for the third exercise that does not exist. Nowhere in the rules described above were you told that you could not go beyond the dots to join them. Of course, in the first two exercises this was not necessary. Your Super Ego, however, invented a 'crap rule' for itself and for your future conduct, based on the experience of the first exercises—namely, that you must 'stay within the dots'!

This may seem a trivial example, with little relevance to the real world. However, think again. How often have you seen managers limiting their actions for fear of breaking a rule that did not exist? How many times have you asked yourself, 'Why didn't I think of that?' The answer will usually lie in the lessons of the above trivial but not trivialising example. Your own Super Ego has screwed you. The value of this exercise is always apparent during my work with organisations. Some people, having seen the answer, use phrases such as 'that's cheating' or 'that isn't common sense'. I have even had 'that's unfair'. All of these are clear indications that the Super Ego is doing its job very thoroughly.

Personal Experience Exercise
$ Think of a time when you missed an opportunity because you did the equivalent of 'not going beyond the dots'.

Managerial life is full of rules; they are an integral part of the process of learning a job. As we have seen, however, the Super Ego will be ready to make more of them than just a way of getting things done. It will be on the look-out for opportunities to turn them into general moral principles that represent the only correct way of behaving. And along with the useful, functional rules of the technology learnt will inevitably come the crap rules that have little to do with achieving results but are the products of the artificial and imaginary constructs of 'how things ought to be' that the Super Ego is so good at inventing. The more training involved in mastering a technology, the higher the likelihood of Super Ego rule-learning taking root. This is what Jürgen Habermas means when he says that technology is conscious forming.[13] This is why doctors think like doctors and accountants think like accountants: their Super Egos have internalised whole ways of thought accumulated during their training.

If a company has a senior manager with an over-zealous commitment to the rules, the results can be disastrous, as the following examples show.

The first concerns a small company which specialised in business development, training and consultancy. Over the previous two years business had been poor as the market had become highly competitive and increasing numbers of businesses had reduced their training budgets during recession. The company's main means of survival during this time had been through the delivery of government-subsidised training rather than the generation of fee-paying customers.

Paul, the General Manager, was fairly intelligent but had a reputation for a fierce temper and an intolerance of anything that diverged from the 'rules'. Realising that the company faced a severe problem, he called a meeting to discuss emergency tactics for survival. He opened the meeting by offering his solutions to the company's problems. These comprised the following:

- Detailed job descriptions for each member of staff (of whom there were only ten!).
- The introduction of an appraisal system.
- A new filing system so that he would know where all

documents were kept (even though the existing system had been considered over-elaborate by all his colleagues).
- A stringent set of performance indicators for the staff.

At no point did he describe ideas for increasing profitability or market share.

Eventually some of his colleagues interrupted to ask why he had ignored their memos containing ideas for new products and services. His response was that he had thrown the memos away because they had not been typed in the 'house style' . . .

Six months after the meeting took place, four people had resigned from the company through low morale and lack of confidence in Paul's leadership. One of these joined a competitor who thrived as a result of implementing the ideas which Paul had rejected. Today Paul has still not completed the strategic plan for the company because he 'can't quite make up his mind on the detail', and the company is continuing to offer the same training programmes despite the fact that this source of business is rapidly drying up.

Another excellent example of a loser is Fraser, a section supervisor at a large life assurance and investment company. Not long ago a team of management consultants was hired to investigate ways of improving productivity. The work was conducted from company headquarters where members of staff worked on the administration of accounts and had no face-to-face contact with customers. Early in their investigations the consultants realised that morale among the administration section was poor and made an appointment with Fraser to discuss possible solutions.

They suggested that Fraser should abolish the rule that all employees must wear a uniform, since this was irrelevant when no customers entered the premises. Fraser was almost apoplectic. For him it signified a 'lack of discipline' and 'decline into anarchy'.

He was even more outraged by the consultants' next suggestion—the introduction of flexitime. Their rationale was quite simple: most of the staff were female and had to take their children to school. Even when they explained to Fraser that this would have a positive impact on productivity, he refused to budge. 'Everyone must be at their desks by 9.00 a.m. every day and that's the rule,' he argued. 'Anyone who arrives after nine is plain lazy and a waste of space.' The consultants soon discovered that high on the list of Fraser's criteria for grading his staff was their time-keeping. Those who arrived at 9 a.m. invariably received an 'excellent' grading, while those who arrived later were penalised, even though their work might be of a higher quality than that of their more punctual colleagues. A year later, while Fraser continues in his restrictive ways, the staff turnover rate has increased by 20 per cent and productivity has declined even further.

When managers are indoctrinated in the expected way of doing the job, the influence of the Super Ego grows. Most professional training is, therefore, malign as it exposes managers to whole sets of imperatives derived from the experiences of others. Thus, the doctor is not concerned with curing patients. He is concerned with applying the rules of curing that he has learnt from the medical school training process. The proven techniques of 'alternative medicine' are not part of that process and, whether they are effective or not, they are to be discounted.

Personal Experience Exercise

$ Can you think of an example when you have met a professional who has been more concerned with the 'ethics' of his profession than with getting things done?

In Britain it is fashionable to ridicule the accountancy profession because its members are considered rigidly conform-ist. Learning to be an accountant is thought to stunt the creative and spontaneous drives of the Id in favour of a passive conformity, heavily dominated by the Super Ego. While this may be an unfair generalisation, it was an accountant who provided me with one of the best examples

I have met of the carry-over of professional training into Super Ego 'crap rule'-based behaviour.

I was recently preparing some presentational material for a lecture to some accountancy students. This comprised a set of overhead projector transparencies to illustrate the major points of my lecture. I was using a variety of coloured pens to draw pictures and write key words in large letters. An accountant saw me doing this and could not resist commenting, 'That isn't very professional!' On being asked for an explanation, he told me that presentations should be in black and white, in text rather than including pictures and, above all, they should be in neat straight lines. I explained that the evidence is that colour, illustration and irregularity imprint themselves onto people's minds more effectively than regular, straight lines of black and white text. My way is shown to produce better learning. 'I still prefer black and white straight lines, they look more professional,' was the man's reply. No doubt neatness and orderly presentation of figures is useful for accountancy. However, this accountant's Super Ego had turned these tools, that are useful in one context, into a generalised rule that is less than effective in another. The incident is worth noting as it demonstrates how people rely on the word 'unprofessional' to justify criticism of someone else's action. Every time the word is uttered there is a crap rule behind it that the Super Ego cannot justify by reference to any other argument.

Personal Experience Exercise
$ Think of the last time you heard someone criticise someone or something as 'unprofessional'. What did this criticism really mean?

THE WINNING MANAGER AND THE TRIAD

I have dwelt at such length on the workings of the human psyche in order to emphasise that the social constraints standing between you and winning the organisation game are artificial and arbitrary. On one hand, you as an individual are driven by forces within you to seek to dominate your environment. These forces want all the goodies the organisation can offer you. They want them with the minimum of effort and they want them now. On the other hand are those in the organisation who are out to impose their rules of conduct upon you. Unfortunately for you, they have a strong ally lurking deep within your own psyche. As I have shown, your own Super Ego is only too ready to conspire with others to constrain you and prevent you from winning the organisation game.

Look about you at those you can identify as losers. Note that they share the characteristic of accepting the rules that others impose on them. Their approach is always to look for approval before acting. They clearly have not heard Saint Francis' views on the matter. He pointed out how much easier it is 'to beg forgiveness rather than to seek permission'. Winning managers get results and sort out the problems, if any, afterwards.

Armed with a knowledge of the way in which the Triad works against your interests, you must compile a new set of rules to govern your behaviour in your managerial life, based, not on the questionable dictates of the Super Egos of others, but upon your own needs. You must rid your Super Ego of the debilitating hindrances of other people's 'morality' and construct a new managerial morality that has your interests at its core.

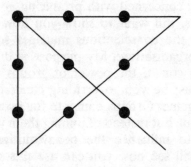

Solution to the problem on p. 37.

3 Joined Up Enemies

'Scotland seems to demand working class heroes who start in the gutter, soar quickly to the heavens and—just as quickly if not quicker—are plunged back into the gutter for the rest of their short lives. Then songs are sung, plays are played, books are commissioned ... it seems we are more at home with failure'.[1] The author of this quote was not a Thatcherite 'Sassenach' but Jimmy Reid, former champion of the under-dog, writing in a recent article about the tendency of many Scots to celebrate the downfall of the successful. Mr Reid's analysis, sadly, is true and should not be confined to Scot-land: winning managers everywhere would be hopelessly naïve if they expected others to support their quest of power. When those others are joined in groups, the message is even stronger. My aim in this chapter is to help you overcome the malevolent influence of groups and use it to your advantage.

YOUR ENEMIES CONSPIRE

Other writers, concerned with producing good little mana-gerial servants, will want to show you how groups can be harnessed by the conscientious manager for the 'general good of the organisation'. My purpose is different. First, I want to warn you of the power of groups to subvert you from what must be your overriding concern—winning the organisation game. Groups compete for possession of your loyalty and soul, but instead of joining them you can harness their power to influence the behaviour and thought of others. You will see how you can use this power for your own ends. Either way, you need to know something about

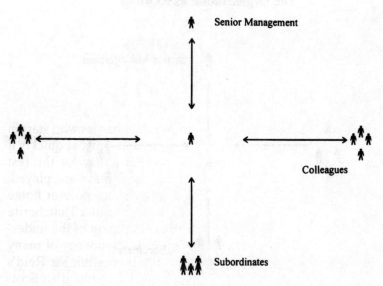

The Organisational Cross

Senior Management

Colleagues

Subordinates

what is referred to in the literature of management as 'group dynamics'.

A quick glance at the organisational cross above will show you that managers in organisations belong to a number of overlapping groups, each exerting influence on their members' behaviour.

The organisation itself will have the character of a group; many of its members, for example, will define themselves in terms of organisational group membership. 'I work for British Rail' tells people something fundamental about the speaker: the employee has imbued a culture that stresses delivery of public service on the deliverer's terms. It also tells the speaker something fundamental about himself: he is a member of a state monopoly whose members see themselves as providing a service to the travelling public. This is why many organisations go to a lot of trouble to foster internal corporate identity with company logos, ties, uniforms and other symbols. As we shall see, groups have

The Organisation as a Group

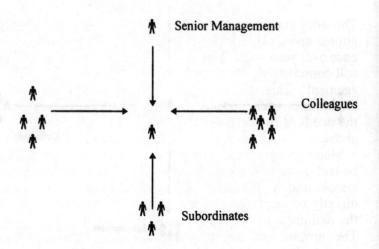

Senior Management

Colleagues

Subordinates

very strong powers of influence over their members and the organisation.

Personal Experience Exercise

$ Think of the organisation in which you work. Do you think of it as just a place where you earn a living or do you feel that you 'belong' to something more than just a place of work?

$ When you talk about what your job is, how soon do you refer to the organisation where you work? Which of the following statements best typifies what you say?

'I work for British Rail.'

'I am an accountant with British Rail.'

'I am an accountant.'

> \$ Can you think of anything your organisation does
>   to make you feel that you are a member of the
>   organisational group?

The story does not end here. Along the arms of the organisational cross, other groups will form and compete for influence over your soul. The formal structure of the organisation
will consciously define a group that may be entitled 'Management'. This will be upwardly orientated, having as its
imperatives such notions as 'managerial prerogative' and
the needs of the organisation as they are passed down from
above.

Membership of this group will be obvious to all. It will
be laid down in the structure of the organisation's reporting
system and its influence will also be overt. It will appeal
directly to the formal loyalty of the individual in terms of
the definition of his or her job in the managerial hierarchy.
The 'upward-looking' structure of the organisation will tell
you 'who belongs to whom' and thus just what organisational
loyalties are expected of you. It will exert formal sanctions
over individuals to induce compliance. But the other dimen-

The Management Group

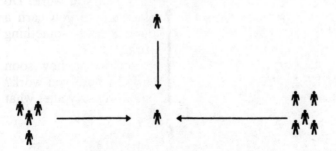

sions of the organisational cross will exert their influence in their own equally powerful ways, and these are not as overt, or as obvious.

Managers in organisations are also members of a downwardly orientated group that consists of those employees who are subordinate to them, who make up their own team. The need to manage subordinates brings you into direct social contact with those who are to be managed.

You will thus be dragged into a group relationship with those upon whom you rely to carry out your job. Not only will you need their support and cooperation in order to do the things that will help you to win, but the very process of group dynamics will influence your behaviour and even your thought process.[2] The power of this group is threefold. First, in order to guide the group towards your goals, you will have to develop a social and managerial relationship with each member. Second, as you work so closely with the group, it can exert significant pressure on you, your thinking and your behaviour. Third, given the specialisation that characterises organisations in terms of the technological division

Your subordinate group

of labour, you are likely to display group prejudices in your attitudes towards those involved in other functions.[3] To put it simply, a marketing manager will share the ways of thought of other marketing specialists in his department and a production manager will think like his fellow engineers. These shared outlooks will make the individuals in groups even more susceptible to group pressures.

Personal Experience Exercise

$ Do you feel that you and your subordinates share some of the mental approaches to your work, while those in other parts of your organisation do not?

$ Can you think of an occasion when you and your subordinates have said derogatory things about other departments in your organisation?

You must also consider the pressure that membership of the *lateral arm* of the organisational cross will exert upon the organisational member. Not only will you be a member of the formal system of the organisation and the formal command structure that is part of it; not only will you be subject to the need to manage people with whom you share both a social relationship and a set of 'professional' perspectives; you will also face the pressures of a 'peer group', others who share your position on the framework of the organisational cross.

Your peer group

This is perhaps the most insidious of the group pressures to which you will be exposed. Your peer group will have norms of group conduct to which you will be expected to conform even though these may undermine your ambitions in the managerial system.

Personal Experience Exercise
$ Have you ever heard anyone being criticised by his peers for being 'too big for his boots', 'getting above himself', 'having ideas above his station'?
$ Can you think of an occasion when someone in your organisation has been ridiculed for dressing too smartly or speaking too well?

From the above description it will be clear that the organisational cross has the characteristic of another instrument of torture: it resembles a rack on which the individual is torn in several directions. The groups that coalesce on its axes are all your enemies, each seeking to pull you towards their own definition of organisational norms, of how you should behave, of how you should think. You may be content with the mere warning of threats to your winning potential. However, this is not enough. You need a more detailed knowledge of group influence.

PEOPLE ARE 'JOINERS'

If you consider the genetic and social development of mankind, it should come as no surprise to learn that man, by his very nature, is a 'joiner'. Humans instinctively want to 'belong' rather than be the 'odd man out'. As pack animals our continued existence on this planet has been determined by our inherited drive towards conformity rather than individuality. The drive towards group orientated behaviour is part of our natural instincts.

If you resent the idea of modern, 'rational man' being reduced to such an evolutionarily deterministic picture, consider the following overview of our genetic history. Our primeval forebears lived or died by their ability to hunt, just like wolves or hyenas, and the individual hunter was clearly an inefficient unit. With his weedy stature and his slowness of foot, he would have been more likely to become the prey of the creatures he hunted. Consider in contrast the effectiveness of Man the pack animal, hunting as a group, combining his innate cunning with that of others to provide food, not just for himself and his family, but for the group. Now ask yourself, 'Whose genes or whose social patterns would be most likely to be passed on to successive generations?' Clearly, in the earliest behaviour of our species, the ability to be part of a group was of vital importance to our survival. Moreover, this ability to be at home as part of a group insured the continuance of our human characteristics, including dependent behaviour.

Now consider the time frame over which such a process of survival of the 'joiner' and his offspring will have been a major factor in passing on group-dependent behaviour. The earliest humanoids are currently thought to have inhabited what is now East Africa around three million years ago. This poor creature went under the unfortunate name of *Homo erectus* but is hardly what we would recognise as a proper ancestor. Let us take a conservative estimate of a million years of human existence as being a more reasonable time frame for the history of our species. Going on from this, in terms of Western civilisation we might take the history of pastoral and latterly settled Man as dating from some five thousand years ago. In contrast, industrialised Man, as we know the species today, has a history of only some two hundred and fifty years. Now translate this into terms of generations who passed on either their genes or their social experience, or a combination of the two, to their offspring. This racial history means that only eight or nine human generations have been free from the direct consequences of the need to form tightly cohesive groups, merely in order to survive and pass on their genes and group-based social structures. For the first *thirty-three thousand* generations of our existence as a species, the propensity to subordinate our individualism to be part of a cohesive group was vital to our existence, and for the next hundred generations, of herdsmen and farmers, it was of equal advantage. To anyone who takes a dispassionate look at our history, it will come as no surprise that we seem to have an in-built and inherited need for group membership; that we behave as pack animals whose behaviour is conditioned by the need to 'belong', to cooperate; that we are driven by the need to conform to the behaviour of the group on whom we depend for mutual survival.

All this may seem to have little relevance to the behaviour of people in modern managerial life. Yet evidence suggests that the imperatives inherited from our past still dominate our behaviour now. The group, in modern organisations, exerts its will over the individual just as strongly as it did over our primeval ancestors. Most often it is an unconscious process, like most of the processes that govern human behaviour, but groups still have power to impose their norms of behaviour on those who would belong, and individuals are still as sensitive to the pressures of group membership as were their primeval forebears.

J. A. C. Brown gives a simple but graphic example of the power of the organisational work group to exact conformity from its members in terms of what might, today, be considered a trivial matter of dress.[4] He quotes the example of the American workman who appeared at his bench sporting a felt hat, what the British call a trilby. In the America of the Fifties this was the dress of the management class, the counterpart of the British bowler hat. The man clearly, as far as his peers were concerned, showed aspirations that were directed not to the 'in-group' of workers, but to the despised 'out-group' of managers. The rules of group dynamics dictated that he had to be brought back into line, in terms of behaviour that was acceptable to the group. The first appearance of the hat caused mild and jocular 'ribbing'. On the second day, when the man continued to wear the 'out-group' symbol, the joking was harsh and of an insulting and punitive nature. On the third day, the man's luncheon box 'went missing'. The message hit home. On the fourth day he came differently attired. The group had made its point. Group norms will be jealously policed and failure to observe them will incur whatever sanctions the group can bring to bear.

Personal Experience Exercise
$ Have you ever felt that you would like to do something but that your colleagues would see this as not being right for 'someone like us'?
$ What sort of punishment would the people around you be likely to hand out to someone who flagrantly failed to conform to what they thought was normal and appropriate behaviour?

This underlines your need as a winning manager to understand the power of groups to influence behaviour. Groups and their dynamics can be both your ally and your deadly enemy. Not only must you be able to use their power for your own ends, you must also be able to see this power for what it is when applied to your own behaviour in the organisation. It is the echo of a primeval past which should not deflect you in your quest to win the organisation game.

IN-GROUPS AND OUT-GROUPS

One of the most salient characteristics of group behaviour is the fact that members will always try to see their group and their fellow members in a positive light. The process of group membership seems to distort the individual's perception of events. A. H. Hastorf and H. Cantril[5] demonstrated this tendency by inviting two groups of American college students, one from Princeton and one from Dartmouth, to view an action replay of a particularly dirty, foul-ridden game of American football between their two universities. Each group was asked to record the blatant fouls committed by either side. While the recording of actual events that was presented to each group was the same, the members of the two groups seemed to perceive the game in totally different ways. The results of the experiment were as follows:

	Princeton Fouls	Dartmouth Fouls
Dartmouth Students	4.4	4.3
Princeton Students	4.2	9.8

It is clear that there was, objectively, only one game. However, what each group of students appeared to experience was two different games. Each was real to them, but clearly distorted so that they saw the group of which they were members in the more favourable light.

If you look at your own organisation you will see the same process at work. Some managers will always find reasons to stand up for their colleagues, even when they are wrong— you may have done so yourself.

The corollary to this positive orientation of members towards the in-group is a negative orientation towards outgroups. In Hastorf and Cantril's experiment, the students' perceptions were coloured both by the partiality of in-group loyalty and by out-group antipathy. In an attempt to observe the latter tendency at work, I watched the behaviour of Scottish and Norwegian students during the televisation of an international soccer match between England and Germany. While the conduct of the observation was different from that of the Hastorf and Cantril study—I was concerned to watch the general behaviour of the spectators—the inference was the same. On one hand, the 'neutral' Norwegian students watched the game with a dispassionate interest in the skill and tactics of both teams, showing a mild partiality for the England team, which was probably based partly upon echoes of the resentment of wartime occupation of Norway by a Nazi-run Germany, but also on the fact that they had been studying in Britain for a number of years and felt some loyalty to what they saw as a home side.

The behaviour of the Scottish group, however, was markedly different. The students cheered every winning move of the German team, even when it was clearly in contravention of the laws of the game. Conversely, every initiative of the out-group, the despised 'Auld Enemy', the English, was raucously booed. To the great embarrassment of the few German students present, each goal by Germany and even each penalty advantage in the German team's favour was greeted by the Scottish group with choruses of *Deutschland über Alles* or the chant of '*Sieg Heil*', complete with Nazi salutes. In-groups clearly need out-groups to sustain and augment the loyalty of their members.

The example of two deadly rival Scottish clubs is a further illustration of this point. The loyalty of the Scottish working classes is divided along lines of support for one of the two great Glasgow teams, Celtic and Rangers. These are more than just football teams, they divide their support along religious, political and, more importantly, social lines. Celtic has its origins amongst the immigrant Irish Catholics who were drawn to Scotland by the prosperity of the Scottish industrial belt. Rangers was the spiritual home of the indigenous Protestant working classes who feared incomers as a threat to their hard-won 'respectability'. Unionism and Protestant ascendancy therefore plays Irish Catholic republicanism and British labourism, alongside the game of football. The divide continues in a symbiotic relationship known as the 'Old Firm'. Each team, however, needs the other to underpin the loyalty of its supporters and, therefore, its continued existence. This was recently made clear by the serious suggestion, when one club was in financial difficulty and faced closure and disbandment, that the other club, despite deep cultural differences, should provide the investment that would ensure its rival's viability as a focus of out-group antipathy.

This tendency for groups to need an out-group to reinforce the loyalty of their members has been shown clearly by the experiments conducted by G. M. Gilbert.[6] These demonstrated the readiness of individuals to define out-groups in a negative light. Gilbert invited the subjects of his experiment to assign items from a list of character traits that defined their perceptions of other national groups.

He found that his subjects were highly consistent in their willingness to define Pirenians, Darians and Wallonians in highly negative terms, even though such groups do not exist and, therefore, could not have formed part of his subjects' experience.

For you as a winning manager the message is clear. The groups into which you will be drawn, as part of your very existence on the managerial playing field, will have all-powerful imperatives that seek to emphasise the in-group's positive characteristics against the out-group's negative ones. Be prepared to use these to your advantage. The mere threat of the other group's advantage over the group that you seek to influence will have the effect of bringing group members into line with the direction that you want them to take. Only the loser, of course, will allow the group to influence his judgement. The perceived negative characteristics of out-groups may be used to mask the very strengths that could make them a threat to the winning manager.

Norman Dixon, in his excellent book *On the Psychology of Military Incompetence*,[7] shows that this tendency of groups to label the members of other groups negatively has, throughout history, produced military losers who underestimated the will-power, determination and ability of their enemies. James Quinn and his colleagues warn business strategists of the group-based propensity to underestimate the opposition by showing how the same process led the German armies of the First World War into a plan that could not bring about victory, but which relied upon the fact that the Western allies, and particularly the French, were 'lesser breeds' who lacked the will and the capability to fight effectively.[8]

Personal Experience Exercise

$ Be honest! Can you think of a group in your organisation whom you would like to see 'done down'?

$ Can you think of an occasion when you have seen this group treated unjustly but have, nevertheless, had a feeling of satisfaction at its treatment?

> $ Can you identify a group of people in your organis-
>   ation against whom you and your colleagues
>   compete?
>
> $ Is there a group in your organisation that you and
>   your colleagues think of as 'a bit of a joke'?
>
> $ Can you think of a time when you were forced to
>   admit that a member of this group had 'done well',
>   despite your expectations about members of his
>   group?

THE UNCONSCIOUS NATURE OF GROUP INFLUENCE

Each group in the organisation will try to gain your loyalty
and conformity to its patterns of behaviour. This can happen
without your knowledge and without your conscious acqui-
escence in the process. Most losers dismiss the idea of group
influence on individuals and believe instead that people act
consciously and rationally.

A more dangerous form of the same delusion lies in your
path if you see yourself as a winning manager: lesser mortals
may be subject to unconscious influence on their behaviour
but you, as a winning type, can stand above it all. All human
beings, however, are subject to the 'rules' of group pressure.
It takes a supreme effort of will to resist and you should be
aware of the threat and take it very seriously indeed. For
this reason I have been at pains to back up my warning with
evidence from experiment. If you are going to stand a
chance of winning in the organisation game, you need a firm
understanding of the power and the insidious nature of the
forces ranged against you. I propose to return later to this
theme, but meanwhile a look at the results of one of the
classic experiments on the power of groups to impose conformity of behaviour, conducted by Muzafer Sherif,[9] will
make the point very forcibly here.

Sherif invited two groups of two or three individuals to
take part in a test, consisting of sitting in a darkened room

and plotting the movement of a single dot on a screen. This is a standard test of individual reaction that is used to select, among others, aeroplane pilots. In Sherif's test, however, the subjects were asked to call out the direction of the movement of the dot on the screen as they observed it.

Tested alone, some individuals will see a large amount of movement in one direction or another as they focus on the dot. Others will see little or no movement depending, among other things, on the reactions of the muscles that control the movement of their eyes. In Sherif's test, the groups came, very quickly, to see the same patterns of movement. After only a few trials they produced a group way of seeing what was happening on the screen.

Of course, what the subjects did not know was that there was no movement at all: the dot remained stationary on the screen. The effort of the eyes to concentrate by focusing and refocusing gave the dot its appearance of movement, known technically as the 'autokinetic effect'. It was this test which ensured that I was not allowed to fulfil my ambition to fly helicopters as an army pilot. My dots zigzagged wildly as my eye muscles sought to catch up with the non-existent movement. What Sherif revealed, by this simple but very effective experiment, was that group influence will cause group members to see the same version of events, even though these events are illusory.

Ignorant of the fact that they had been duped by the autokinetic effect and exposed to group influence, the subjects went back to being tested individually. The recurring theme was that even when tested individually each person continued to report the dot movement as seen by the group. Their perception of physical events had been distorted towards a common group norm.

As we shall see later, there is ample experimental evidence to show that this is a marked feature of group power over its members. Whether you like it or not, your perception of events is coloured by the group perception of the world and you are not the independent, rational individual you imagine yourself to be.

Personal Experience Exercise
$ Can you think of a time when you have moved from one organisation to another, or from one part of an organisation to another, and suddenly found yourself seeing things in a different light?

FACILITATION AND INHIBITION

Of course, membership of a group can also have highly positive results. Over and above the overt and commonsense notions of 'team spirit' and 'we are all in this together', the mere presence of others, engaged with us in the same activity, seems to contribute to increased performance, greater output and productivity. I am old enough to remember when Dr Roger Bannister overcame the great psychological barrier of running the mile in under four minutes, a feat that people had said was impossible. But he did not do it alone. As he ran round the Iffley Road track in Oxford, he had Christopher Chattaway with him as a pace-maker. The presence of Chattaway spurred the record-breaker on to even greater efforts. This phenomenon of 'social facilitation', of the presence of others increasing performance, appears to be built into the behaviour of groups and can be observed over a number of species engaged in a variety of activities.

F. H. Allport[10] conducted several experiments which showed how this process of social facilitation influenced humans. He found that students, given the task of crossing out the vowels in a piece of text, performed markedly more effectively when the exercise was carried out in the company of others similarly occupied. Further, he showed that this process, combined with another characteristic of groups—the ability of the ideas of one group member to spark new ideas in the mind of another[11]—could increase the productivity of groups who were set the task of producing 'bad ideas'.

Harry F. Harlow[12] found that rats in a group will feed at a greater rate of intake. This was not related to competition for food, merely to the presence of other rats engaged in the same activity. S. C. Chen[13] noticed that ants built faster as a group than when working alone. Knut Larsson[14] observed the behaviour of rats copulating. He found that, in the company of other couples engaged in sexual activity, male rats produced more ejaculations per minute than they did when couples copulated alone. Again using rats, E. Ramussen[15] showed that social facilitation caused the animals to drink more in the presence of other rats than on their own. Even when they had to endure electric shocks from their drinking water, the effect of social facilitation still induced greater intakes of liquid. Any drinker in a British pub will know that a pint of beer seems to last only a fraction of the time when drunk in company as opposed to being drunk in solitude. This is why British pub landlords love the practice of 'round buying'!

Personal Experience Exercise
$ Can you think of a time when a difficult job suddenly seemed easier because there were other people around you doing the same task?

All this is meant to demonstrate to you the power that groups exert over their members. Harnessed to the right ends, groups can be a very effective weapon in your winning armoury. If you can learn to control their power, you can become more productive than when attempting to work alone, and those of you who naturally fear the power of your group of subordinates can be reassured: instead of fearing them, realise that, once your goals are clear, groups can be more effective than isolated individuals in helping you realise your aims.

The opposite effect of facilitation by groups is one of inhibition. Under certain circumstances, the presence of others will act as a brake upon action rather than facilitating it. B. Latané and J. Darley[16] set up an experiment that demonstrated this clearly. They invited young male students to take part in an experiment to test their perception. They were asked to report, either alone or in pairs, to the room where the experiment was to take place. There they were met by a young female assistant who asked them to wait while she went next door to fetch the test material. They heard the sound of her entering the adjacent room and placing a ladder against the wall, followed by a crash and the girl's plaintive moans of, 'Oh God, my foot! I can't move.' Then silence. At the end of two minutes, if no one had come to the rescue, the participants heard the sound of the assistant limping and dragging her foot down the corridor.

The experiment, of course, had nothing to do with perception. The purpose of Latané and Darley was to observe the reaction of the young gallants, alone or when accompanied. The results were extremely interesting for those concerned with the effects of groups on human behaviour. When the students were alone, the first man to react took about ten seconds to make up his mind to go to the aid of the damsel in distress. By the time thirty seconds had elapsed, sixty per cent of lone students had decided to investigate the trouble. By the end of the experiment, seventy per cent had ventured into the next room to help.

When two students were left waiting together, however, *twenty* seconds elapsed before the first pair sallied forth to the rescue. After that, fewer and fewer students moved to help so that, by the end of the experiment, when the young woman assistant limped off, only forty per cent of participating groups had stirred themselves to action. The remaining sixty per cent were content to remain in the waiting room looking at each other, each made inert by the other's presence.

You can learn much about group psychology from this simple experiment. Although groups may perform better than individuals when they have a set of aims or goals, faced with new or unexpected situations, where there is no group norm to dictate behaviour, the presence of other people will act as a brake. The normal human reaction of the majority of lone students was to go to the aid of the assistant. When others were present, individuals needed a group 'OK' before

taking action, and even after two minutes this was still not
forthcoming for the majority of them. Groups need a cata-
lyst to action, otherwise inertia and inaction are likely to
dominate their behaviour. This is borne out by studies of
how juries behave in legal trials: the first person to speak is
likely to be elected foreman.[17] You should therefore make
sure you fill the vacuum produced by an indecisive group as
you can then direct it towards your own agenda.

Personal Experience Exercise
$ Have you ever watched a group of people standing
around, waiting for someone to take the lead? Did
you notice how they were galvanised into action?

GROUP PRESSURE AND ATTITUDES

In looking at the autokinetic phenomenon we saw how
groups can influence their members' perception of the world
about them. In order to underline the detrimental effects of
groups on individuals' behaviour, let's examine some experiments on the effect of group pressure. The most famous
series of these was carried out by Solomon Asch[18] who
invited groups of six to eight American college students to
take part in an experiment on perception. By now the reader
will rightly smell a rat, for the experiments were not all that
they seemed. Ostensibly, the task of each group was to
observe a vertical line on a card and then to say which of
three lines shown on a second card matched the first line
for length. Done 'for real', this was an extremely easy task,
with less than a one per cent chance of individuals making
an error.

The first round of the experiment started in a relaxed
style, with the participants being asked in turn to identify
by number the line from the second card that matched the
first. The test was so easy that there was no disagreement.
The second round proceeded in the same manner and the

participants settled down to what seemed to be another boring experiment.

When it came to the third trial there was an unexpected change in the routine: a student disagreed with the selections that the others had made. He seemed bewildered. On the next trial he was again the odd man out in his choices. He became more and more anxious and hesitant in speaking up as he stood out as the only dissenter in succeeding trials. This pattern was repeated with each group of students.

What the one harassed individual did not know was that he was the only one relying on his own perceptions to attempt the task. He was a stooge. The other participants had been scripted to play roles as part of an experiment to demonstrate the effect upon conformity that results from group pressure to present the wrong answer. And very interesting those results were. Using this simple method, Asch was able to induce his stooges to produce the group 'wrong' answers along with the group in thirty-seven per cent of trials—this in a test where mistakes are almost impossible when played for real.

In some of his experiments Asch tried to gauge the strength of group pressure by giving the stooge an ally who would choose the correct solution. He found that, while the stooge's errors were reduced, there was still a marked tendency for the group's imposed solution to make the stooge conform. The clear explanation of these experiments is that individuals find it difficult and distressing to disagree with the group.

After the experiments, Asch interviewed the conformers to try to find out what made them bow to group pressure. Their explanations produced three common themes. First, there were those who admitted that they knew they were wrong but did not want to stand out from the majority. Here we have an example of a dangerous loser trait that values fitting in with the group, even when it comes to such a small matter as disagreeing about the length of some lines on a piece of card. Another group claimed that they were not sure what the correct answer was and so they went along with the majority. Here, in a test that presented little problem when carried out without the influence of a group, these individuals had been made to doubt their own judgement. For them, when there was doubt, the majority had to be right. The third category really showed the insidious power of groups over their members. These individuals genuinely thought that they had reported what they had seen. On them the group influence had worked its spell, so that their perceptions became distorted. After what was after all a very mild exposure to the pressure of united group opinion, they actually came to see what the group claimed to see.

Personal Experience Exercise
$ Think of a time when you found yourself the only one in a group to disagree with what appeared to be the majority view on something. How did you feel?
$ Have you ever seen someone 'give in' to group pressure, even when it was clear that the group was totally wrong?

This last finding of Asch's experiment is the most difficult to accept. You have probably met those who are happy to go along with the majority for a quiet life, and you may also be prepared to admit that there are those about you who are so insecure as to doubt their own judgement enough to give the group the benefit of the doubt. But the idea that an individual might be so brainwashed by the group's collective distortion of objective events is hard for us, with our faith in human rationality, to swallow. Surely, Asch's conformers cannot have been telling the truth when they reported their motivation for going along with the group. Surely, they must have been people of low intelligence and of low moral fibre.

To deal with these doubts I recreated Asch's experiment using, not callow youths drawn from a population of American college students, but British army officers. My stooge was a major with a good university degree and a decoration for bravery, who had been chosen for a career path that would lead him to a potentially high rank. The accomplices were a group of similar officers, of both sexes. In my experiment, the accomplices were invited, not merely to conform to a script but to ad lib with barracking of a punitive nature when the stooge deviated from the group's responses. My experiment also required the stooge to record his decision on paper, before the group delivered its verdict on each trial, so as to be able to trace what he actually thought he saw as opposed to what he said he saw. The experiment was video-taped.

The result nearly cost me a friendship. It certainly cost me a bottle of champagne as a consolation to the stooge, for he followed the pattern of Asch's third group of conformers after only a few trials. At first he held out against the group. Against a torrent of abuse, which included verbal assaults upon his sexual orientation and his manhood, he began to record one observation but declare the group's version publicly. After a short while, however, he began to record the distorted 'group' solution, even before the group had made its views public. This leader of men, genuine winning manager material by anybody's standards, had his perception subverted by the power of the group to exert conformity to its perception. The video-recording proved to be very instructive. It was clear that the poor stooge felt himself to be under extreme pressure. He squirmed in his seat. He twisted his hair. He even put his hands over his ears as if to shut out the influence of the group, all to no avail. In the end, he conformed to the group's perceptions, even over the trivial matter of the length of lines on a piece of card.

One last doubt about the effects of group pressure needs to be cleared up. Asch's experiments dealt only with the simple matter of disagreement about the length of lines. While they certainly showed the strength of group pressure to conform, they did not deal with the group's power to influence more fundamental matters, such as ideas. This dimension was addressed by Richard Crutchfield,[19] who carried out a series of experiments to see how far a group could bring about conformity when the issue was one of political opinion.

First he chose his participants by their political orientation. He gave groups of students a questionnaire which placed them on a left/right political continuum. He then selected those students whose answers showed them to be liberal or left in their opinions. Next, he collected a series of statements from the political literature of current affairs. He chose ideas from left-wing, neutral and right-wing sources and from these he constructed the material that he showed to his test groups. This consisted of questions with a choice of answers. For example:

The greatest problem facing the USA today is:

    a Recession.
    b Educational facilities.
    c Subversive activities.
    d Mental health.
    e Crime and corruption.

Using a method based on Asch's work, but more efficient in that each individual was isolated from the rest of the group by language laboratory-type booths, his groups were given the statements and invited to push a button against the statement with which they most agreed. In fact, the group solutions were rigged to show a preference for the one solution that had been included from right-wing literature. In the above example, Crutchfield succeeded in using the power of purported group pressure to make forty-eight per cent of his left-wing subjects agree with a statement taken from the literature of the extreme right-wing Johr Birch Society, despite the presence in the list of several more natural choices for people with left-wing views. He clearly made the point that even people's ideas are vulnerable to the pressure of group norms.

GROUPS AND THE WINNING MANAGER

We have spent a lot of time outlining the results of the experiments into group pressure on the behaviour and even the thinking of individuals, because an understanding of the power of groups is vital to you if you are to be a winner in the organisation game. If you insist on blundering on, believing in the power of the individual to plough his own furrow while disregarding the influence of others, then you will miss much in the way of opportunity. More importantly, you will fail to see some of the traps that your own inherited psychological make-up has laid for you to make you into a loser. You need to learn to see groups and their influence both as potential sources of power and as serious obstacles to your winning.

First, there is the power that groups can exert over others. If you can tap that power by dominating the process that defines, makes and then enforces the group way of seeing the world, then you have the potential to achieve your ends. If you can gain control of the group by winning the compliance of an effective proportion of its members, the group will use its influence on your behalf.

But also remember the power of groups to influence you. I hope you will have seen from the above experiments that you, however strong your personality, are subject to the magic that groups work on their members to gain compliance. And the groups that inhabit the organisation are out to drag you into their ways—losers' ways. Remember too that your own built-in 'traitor within'—your Super Ego—is also on the look-out for new rules to add to its repertoire and will be only too ready to internalise the norms of the group and so limit your behaviour. The groups to which you will be exposed in the organisation game will clearly have different sets of norms to which they will try to tie you. Some are easily dealt with; others are made more insidious by their strength combined with their transparency. Armed with the maps of groups as they form on the organisational cross (see pp. 46–9), you will be able to identify for yourself the type of pressure that each group is likely to bring to bear on you. Let me deal with two of the groupings, whose influence is likely to be less overt and therefore more insidiously influential on your behaviour.

First, the organisation itself will have a corporate culture which will form the basis for expectations about the behaviour of its members. Long exposure to the practices of the organisation will have stuffed the Super Egos of those about you with a high regard for particular ways of doing the organisation's business. This will become tied in with notions of professionalism, of the importance of style rather of achieving outcomes. The incomer to an organisation will soon learn that it is the way in which he achieves results that counts, not the outcomes themselves. My colleague Eleanor Shaw and I observed this process in operation in the workings of a university department which was anxious to achieve a change of status, to move from being a mere university department to becoming a 'Business School'. The department's way of conducting business was to set up a committee, to prepare a carefully argued report, and then to approach the decision-making bodies of the university for the relevant action. Bored with this laborious procedure, I went straight to the power authorities with, first, an oral case for the change and then a short synopsis of the general arguments. The change was immediately welcomed at the highest level. The influential old hands of the department, however, rather than applauding the political handling of the outcome, complained that the approach was unprofessional and that the 'proper procedures' had not been followed. In this case, the group culture was one that valued outcomes only if the requisite amount of talk, paper and demonstrated hard graft had been expended in order to achieve them. These were, of course, losers' ways which were aimed at shaping the behaviour of others.

The second group on the Organisational Cross map of which you must beware is that of your peers. J. A. C. Brown[20] makes the point strongly that groups expect their members to conform to their ways of behaving in the most minute detail. His example of the workman and his hat, quoted earlier, is highly relevant here. Brown's point is that peer groups have very strong rules about individual behaviour that does not conform to their conceptions of how 'people like us' behave. Attempts to adopt the style and behaviour of other groups, particularly of groups thought to be superior, are seen as rejections of the in-group code of solidarity. Thus, Brown's felt-hatted workman was seen as trying to reject the group in favour of a group above his own, to which he did not and should not belong. The problem for you as a potential winner is that winning entails moving out of lower, less prestigious groups to join higher groups where more of the organisation's 'goodies' are to be gained. Indeed, part of the winning process entails anticipating the characteristics of the group to which you aspire by behaving in ways that signal membership of the target group. From this point of view, the junior manager who aspires to be a director is best advised to adopt the dress, behaviour and the general life-style of a director. The junior lecturer who wants to be a professor needs to behave like a professor. The priest who wants to be a bishop is advised to behave episcopally. Advancement and preferment are more likely to fall to those who demonstrate their behavioural suitability for promotion early, rather than waiting for promotion before becoming socialised into the senior group's way of doing things in the organisation.

This principle runs counter to the rules of group behaviour. As we have seen, groups expect their members to follow the group's centre of gravity of behaviour. As a good group member, you remain in the 'public bar', adhering to public bar dress and etiquette, until called to the 'saloon bar'. But the peer group to which you belong is, by nature, a group of losers. While it contains tomorrow's winners, the majority of its members will be those who cannot or will not move onwards and upwards; they will have a psychological stake in seeing others lose with them. It is this group that will seek to influence you to remain in its grip, until the sheer force of ability drags you upwards. It is this group that will be ready to use all the sanctions that groups can bring to bear to stop you from seeking to fulfil your potential.

If you really want to win you need to see groups for what they are—your enemies. They are the products of an inherited past that may have ensured your ancestors' survival but are now, like your appendix, an irrelevant threat to *your* survival. You owe nothing to anyone, least of all to those about you in the organisation. By all means pay lip-service to group membership—so much is necessary for day-to-day survival—but realise that any loyalty you may feel for them is taken for granted and, in terms of helping you towards your goal, is unlikely to receive any reward.

4 Organisations as Your Enemy

I began this book with a warning that the path to winning would not be at all smooth. Along the way lurk enemies who, by their very nature, are out to destroy your ambition and turn you into a loser. One of these is the organisation itself. I repeat my earlier warning that the needs of the organisation are at odds with your interests. The organisation is out to exploit you. It therefore follows that you need to know how organisations go about their business, how they draw themselves together to prevent you from winning.

You may ask why, having dealt with people in groups, you have to consider organisations. Surely, they are made up of people in groups. Should not the warnings of the previous chapter be enough? The answer is that organisations seem to take on characteristics that are different from the mere sum of the individuals or even the groups that make them up. They have a power to which individuals do not have access, drawn from three sources:

1 The synergy of individual people and groups working together towards a similar set of related purposes makes the organisation more powerful than the sum of the actions of its members.
2 Organisations can use their size for tasks that individuals or groups of individuals alone could not achieve. They stand apart from time and space and are able to operate in many locations simultaneously.
3 They are not dependent upon individuals. People may come and go, but the organisation itself carries on in more or less the same way as it has always done. It is like the proverbial hammer that has had four handles and three

heads: its parts may change over time but it remains the same organisation.

For these reasons, we speak of organisations as though they were entities in their own right, as though they had an individuality and a consciousness of their own—for example, the Army or British Airways. They therefore require special consideration, not only because they provide the environment of the game in which you are a player, but because they represent a powerful and special sort of enemy.

Why have organisations become so powerful? The answers to this question are vital: they will enable you to attain your goals even though the organisation may try to prevent you from doing so. As with groups, organisations have strengths to pull individuals into their field of gravity, against the latters' interests. Above all, you need to realise that you must apply to organisations the same rules about loyalty that you apply to groups. Organisations are there for you to use for your own purposes and you need to learn to use them. You must learn how to get what you want from them whilst giving the minimum in return. Shed any of the losers' notions about loyalty that may lurk in the depths of your Super Ego. Organisations represent nothing more than arbitrary constructions that can be used to help you or hinder you in your quest to win.

Personal Experience Exercise

$ Would it seem at all odd to you if you overheard someone speaking of an organisation as though it were a real person, saying something like, 'General Motors thinks it will make a bigger profit next year'?

$ Take a look at your own organisation. Despite the many comings or goings of the people within it over the last year, how far has it remained recognisably the same?

$ Think of someone in your organisation who is regarded as a loyal and reliable member. What does he or she seem to get in return?

$ Be honest! How much loyalty do you think you feel towards your organisation?

$ What would have to take place to change the degree of loyalty that you feel towards your organisation, in either direction?

THE ANATOMY OF ORGANISATIONS

A convenient place to start any study of organisations and the way they operate is to look at what the German writer, Max Weber, had to say about them.[1] His careful analysis will enable you to protect yourself from the exploitative power that organisations have over you and to formulate your plan to fight back and win.

As with the work of Freud, Weber's terminology needs some special explanation. For instance, he used the term 'bureaucracy' to describe the way modern organisations 'organise' themselves. The name is problematic since it is often used as a term of abuse. For example, an entry in Hansard for 1968[2] shows a House of Commons motion condemning 'the continued growth of bureaucracy', by which was meant the growth of frustrating regulations and 'red tape'. It is a clear warning to anyone who harbours sympathy for organisations and their works that the term 'bureaucracy' has come to mean, in everyday language, blundering inefficiency and the proliferation of seemingly meaningless procedures and regulations that hinder the achievement of managerial outcome. Nevertheless, Weber did not mean this. He used the term without any of its pejorative connotations, merely to describe the way organisations put themselves together, and his analysis offers a convenient vocabulary for explaining what is going on in the organisation about you.

His description is particularly helpful to you as it looks at the topic from the perspective of power: he was concerned to show how organisations and the managers in them come to have power over others. Since you will need to learn how to resist, modify and subvert that power, this exposure is a highly valuable piece of 'battle field intelligence'. Weber's starting point was that modern organisations, 'bureaucracies', are based upon what he called 'rational/legal' authority. Unlike the institutions of feudalism or revolutionary government, they exercise power over their members through a perceived 'legitimacy'. They act, not on the whim of the ruler of the 'party', but according to carefully conceived sets of rules that are accepted as legitimate by those to whom they apply and persuade them to perform as instructed.

In Weber's view, organisations operate through a system of 'office-holders', each exercising his or her authority according to the rules, backed up by a filing system that records actions and tells office-holders what the organisation has done in the past, in similar situations. This he sees as their source of strength.

The basic building blocks of a bureaucracy are 'offices', arranged in a hierarchy along what Henri Fayol[3] referred to as a 'scalar chain', a clearly laid down set of specialist responsibilities so arranged as to leave no gap in authority. Each office-holder's power to act is carefully circumscribed by the formal 'rules' of the organisation. Unlike the appointments made under other systems—inherited office, nepotism, party placements—bureaucracies select their office-holders by qualification in the shape of training and experience. Once in the system, it is usual for office-holders to aspire to progress up the hierarchy of offices, or move to higher offices in other, similar organisations.

If this system seems self-evident to you, note that, until 1870, commissions and promotion in the British Army were bought. As recently as 1990 a commission had to be set up to weed out from the former East German university system the professors who had been appointed not on academic merit, but because of their Party connections. The key to understanding the notion of office in modern organisations is that its holders are professionals in two senses. Not only do they hold office because of their qualifications, but their qualifications are their sole claim to office, and the office provides their livelihood, status and even definition of their relative status in society as a whole.

Personal Experience Exercise

$ Can you identify the scalar chain of offices, from top to bottom, in your organisation?

$ Where does the office you hold sit on the chain?

$ Could you move up the chain and, if so, what would you need to do?

$ How well would you survive financially if you were not in your current office?

$ Are there equally rewarding 'offices' to be had easily elsewhere in other organisations?

Weber showed that bureaucracies are effective. They get things done in a way that other forms of organisation, or individuals acting alone, cannot. By a process of natural selection, therefore, the bureaucratic system has become the norm in all advanced societies, from the commercial or industrial enterprises of advanced capitalism to the state apparatuses of communist countries. Its effectiveness lies in the control that it wields over its members. The notion of professionally qualified office-holders ensures the right training and background at all levels in the hierarchy. Because each office-holder is hemmed in by the rules of the organisation, bureaucracies can delegate action to the right level of competence and conserve the energies of other levels in their hierarchy for other appropriate tasks. Charles Perrow's notion of organisational eunuchs is again relevant here. The trained 'professional' is unlikely to think of doing anything but the tasks that the organisation expects of him. His Super Ego has been filled with the rules of 'correct' managerial behaviour through the training he has received to do his job. The 'wrong' managers are kept out of office and even out of the organisation by selection processes[4] which emphasise 'fitting in'—not questioning the way the organisation conducts its business.[5]

If one office-holder leaves, another trained person takes his place. The newcomer merely 'slots in', armed with his training, his knowledge of the formal rules and his access to the 'collective memory' of the organisation—the files recording how things have been done in the past. Weber saw these qualities as giving bureaucracies two things that made them more effective than other forms of organisation. They are reliable: managers come and go but office-holders continue to carry out the functions of their offices. They are also disciplined: they can control their members and constrain them to do just what the organisation wants them to do, according to its rules.

From this you can see that organisations have considerable power over your life. They set out the agenda for what you must do to survive in them. They set and police the limits of what you can and cannot do. And, by the control of resources, they control what you can have as an organisational member.

Their power also extends beyond their members. Those who seek action from an organisation must rely on the good will of its office-holders to get what they need from it. The latter, with time and knowledge on their side and the power to grant or withhold what the organisation has to offer, will always be a match for individuals.[6]

Personal Experience Exercise

$ Think of a time when you have moved to a new job, a new office. How did you find out what you were supposed to do in that office?

$ What about your current office? Can you identify what you are expected to do without seeking permission from your boss?

$ Can you think of things which you dare not do without referring upwards for permission?

$ Have you ever felt that you needed to 'keep in' with someone, just in order to get what you needed from the office that he controlled?

FEET OF CLAY

Although modern bureaucratic organisations appear to be effective at first sight, in reality they are potentially highly inefficient. The very characteristics that make them so powerful also contribute to inefficiency and indeed ineffectiveness. Moreover, from your point of view, the way that they are constructed is inimical to your goal of winning the organisation game. Bureaucracies have the power to constrain their managers; the hierarchies on which they are built frustrate your need to pursue your winning agenda. The rules governing the actions of the office-holders hedge your interests and are all the more powerful and insidious because they operate largely at an unconscious level. They are so much part of the everyday life of organisations that they are taken for granted as being the natural and normal order of things.

Faced with this all-pervading power you must be able to challenge and reject it; you need to learn to stand back from the rules and expectations of your office and see bureaucracy for what it is—your enemy. As we have seen, a major advantage that bureaucratic organisations have in the exercise of control is that they are perceived as legitimate by those who inhabit them, because of their impersonality and reference to the 'rules'. They claim and receive the loyalty of their members on this basis, and within the system the holders of superior office likewise claim and receive the loyalty of those below them in the scalar chain. Over and above this formal legitimacy, the processes of group loyalty draw individuals into a psychological bond with the organisation that reinforces the loyalties of the hierarchy.

You must see this legitimacy as flawed and be prepared to fight it. From your point of view, the power of the organisation is illegitimate because it stands between you and your goal of being a winning manager. Of course that power may be real, with real implications for the behaviour of individuals subjected to it, and you are certainly advised to feign your acceptance of its absolute legitimacy. Internally, however, you must recognise and spurn it as the imposition of someone else's rules upon your life, upon your need to win.

One of your problems is that, throughout all of our lives, the notion of loyalty to organisations has been stuffed into our Super Egos. Because of this, we find it extremely difficult even to think disloyal thoughts about the organisations to which we belong. We may feel frustrated by the lumbering inefficiencies of bureaucracy; we may even be angry at the way we and other managers are treated. Nevertheless, our Super Egos have learnt that we must respect organisations, that we must give them our loyalty, that we must recognise their legitimate right to exercise power over us. These are losers' rules and you, as a winning manager, need to substitute for them a new set of attitudes to organisations in which they are seen not merely as your enemies, but as enemies that are to be despised rather than respected.

The nature of the way bureaucratic organisations work in practice makes this easier than you might think. Over and above their illegitimacy as obstacles to your getting your way, they are illegitimate in terms of their own claim to their members' loyalty—its very basis is a sham. Organisations are no more than vehicles for other managers to impose their vision of the world upon you. Hidden behind the façade of the impersonal and altruistic 'office' is the office-holder with his own personality and goals. The seeming objective and impersonal rules are therefore merely the product of other managers' pursuit of their own ends, and the illusion of legitimacy derives from the fact that these ends are most often rooted in those managers' Super Egos and not necessarily in pursuit of their perceived personal advantage. However, as we have seen, Super Egos are full of crap rules that only a loser can take seriously. Organisations are not the impersonal altruistic entities that their members would have you believe: they are battlegrounds for power. Realise this, free yourself from misplaced loyalties, and you will be able to make a bid for a share of that power.

The German writer Robert Michels showed how office-holders bring their own goals to the workings of organisations and impose them upon other members through the power of their offices. He looked at the workings of the German socialist parties and trade unions before the First World War[7] and studied organisations that had been set up with the express aim of bettering the lot of German working-class people. The nature of the offices that made up these organisations, however, inevitably meant that they were filled by managers drawn from the educated middle classes, rather than by manual workers. These brought to their work middle-class perspectives based upon what middle-class intellectuals of the time thought the working classes ought to have, rather than what working-class people might have chosen as goals. Thus, instead of bettering the lot of the poor by working within the existing capitalist system, they preoccupied themselves with socialist ideology. What went on in these organisations had more to do with the retention of office and power for the office-holders than with the stated aim of helping the 'underdog'.

This process is still at work today, and not only in Germany. The leaders of the British Trades Union movement spend a great deal of the time promoting the cause of socialism in general and the Labour Party in particular, although in successive general elections the majority of their members have voted for non-socialist parties. For example, much of the behaviour of the mine workers' union in the 1980s could only be explained in terms of the leadership's vision of the miners as an 'élite vanguard' in the fight against capitalism in general and a Conservative government in particular.[8] That this concern with political ideology was not shared by ordinary union members is borne out by the refusal of the leaders of the National Union of Mine Workers to obey union rules and hold a vote before calling a strike in their battle with the government in 1983, on the grounds that the 'membership could not be trusted'.

Trades union leaders are not alone when it comes to applying their own agendas that have little to do with the needs of those whom they are supposed to serve. Anyone familiar with the workings of the British National Health Service will recognise the cynic's description of it as 'run by nurses for the British Medical Association'. The rules of the system, which has as its formal stated goal 'the provision of health care for the taxpayer', are better explained as being about the maintenance of the status and power of doctors against other medical professions and the provision of treatment to the customer on the medical professions' own terms.

Personal Experience Exercise

$ If you have a British National Insurance card, look at the back. Note that before you can change your supplier—your doctor—you need to get his or her written permission!

$ Think of a visit you have had to a British state hospital. Did you feel that you were a valued customer or client or that you were treated at best as a mere 'case'?

$ When you have had a hospital appointment, did you see a doctor at the appointment time or did you have to wait along with a mass of other patients who had the same block booking?

$ Have you ever felt that the behaviour of a doctor towards you was off-hand, high-handed or patronising? Did you dare to comment?

BUREAUCRATS

One of the claims to legitimacy made by organisations is that they are there to get a job done. Hospitals are there to cure people, universities are supposed to collect knowledge and pass it on to their students, armies train to defend the nation. If you are unconvinced by the argument that organisational goals are subverted by office-holders bringing their own definitions to the organisation, try another test of legitimacy by asking the question, 'How far do the rules that govern the conduct of an organisation lead to the formal stated aim?'

Weber's 'ideal type'[9] picture of bureaucracies looks good on paper. It sees organisations as having a clearly defined code of conduct—the rules—which ensures that everyone in the organisation knows what he has to do and what he may not do. Surely this should guarantee that members complete the appropriate tasks that contribute to the purpose of the organisation. This approach, however, does not take into account the way managers behave when they take over offices.

The problem with the rules, as they apply to managerial offices and office-holders, is that they allow for a confusion between ends and means in the minds of the managers who operate them. In order for the organisation to do its job, the overall task must necessarily be broken down into smaller tasks that are manageable by individuals. Rules are therefore set out to govern the conduct of each part of the overall task, as Max Weber has pointed out. Individual office-holders become responsible for their own small part of the task and have the responsibility to see that it is carried out 'according to the rules'. And herein lies the problem. The rules take on a meaning for the office-holder, which they were never meant to have. They become divorced from their original function of helping to fulfil the task of the organisation and become ends in themselves, part of the Super Ego repertoire of the office-holder who, from the narrow perspective of his office, is unconcerned with the effects that the application of the rules might have on the job of the organisation. Important managerial opportunities may be missed, the organisation may fail in its primary task—so be it. The rules, as they apply to the office-holder's small patch of activity, must be observed, for in his mind they somehow stand above such material considerations as 'getting the job done'. To such managers, and there are lots of them about, managerial life is an art form; outcomes are less important than the ways of achieving them and can only be achieved legitimately by application of the organisation's rules or not at all.

In itself all this would be bad enough. However, as we have seen from examining the workings of the Super Ego, managers are not content with the rules that are served up to them. Rather than looking for an excuse to avoid the rules, they have an urge to extend existing rules to cover even doubtful cases that could have been slipped through in order to get the job done. What Robert Merton[10] describes as the 'bureaucratic personality' seeks to look behind the letter of organisational law to find a spirit that may not exist outside the office-holder's own desire to apply rules for their own sake. For such managers the organisation offers an ideal field for the exercise of personal power. Their role as guardians of the rule book gives them a self-importance that seems to compensate for their otherwise stunted and unfulfilled personal existence and becomes a way of life. While they may see themselves as loyal servers of the good of the organisation, you must recognise them for what they are—losers who get in the way of managerial effectiveness.

This process is particularly prevalent where the office-holder is the sort of professional who learns rules outside the organisation and looks outward to a corpus of professional conduct for legitimation, rather than concentrating on the organisation and its task. Two such cases spring to mind and illustrate how dangerous such managers can be.

A large public sector organisation had the chance of landing a prestigious and lucrative contract. Because of its elaborate decision-making procedures, the deadline for appointing the staff to do the work was reached. There was a highly qualified candidate who was willing to take up the post at short notice. However, the organisation's self-imposed personnel policy stipulated two weeks of advertisement for certain grades of employee, followed by two weeks' notice for short-listed candidates and the formal interview of a choice of candidates short-listed—a delay of some five weeks. This procedure did not explicitly apply to the class of employee sought, but despite the urging of senior management, the personnel department insisted upon following it. The deadline for the contract was missed. Only by luck, and no thanks to those who put their interpretation of the organisation's rules above all else, the deadline for the appointment was extended and the intended candidate took the post. At no time did the personnel professionals feel they had jeopardised the organisation's good or that they had wasted a great deal of managerial time in the process. Rather, they felt a self-righteous satisfaction in having followed the 'rules'.

The second example is even more absurd. A number of strict safety rules govern the handling of military ammunition, one of these calling for two empty trucks to sit between the locomotive and ammunition trucks when ammunition is transported by rail. A typical ammunition train will be broken into four sections for shunting in an ammunition depot. Each section will be pushed or pulled by a locomotive from either end. This means that sixteen empty trucks are required for every ammunition train. Since trucks have to be hired at a rate that doubles every day, the bill for trucks tied up while trains are unloaded, sometimes for a week at a time, adds thousands of pounds a year to the bill paid by the taxpayer. When a staff officer attempted to cut this bill his efforts were greeted with horror by those concerned with safety. It was pointed out that the bill was being incurred for conditions which no longer apply. The 'spacer' trucks were there to stop sparks from the engine falling on the black powder in open trucks. Diesel locomotives produce no sparks; modern ammunition does not use black powder and is not ignited by fire; the trucks in which ammunition is transported are closed. Nevertheless, the rules of safety are sacrosanct. It is not the job of safety officers to consider the cost to the taxpayer of the rules and their observance.

The propensity for office-holders to make the rules of their office into a moral imperative exists in all organisations. It will be stronger the farther away the office-holder is from being financially accountable for his actions. Nevertheless, Midge Hobsworf—'Sorry, mate, it's more than m'job's worth'—is alive and well and all about you in managerial life. In small 'for profit' organisations, this bureaucratic personality will soon be recognised for what it is, a hindrance to getting things done and, therefore, a financial liability. In larger organisations, with their diffused responsibilities and their proliferation of dark corners in which individuals can hide to escape notice, Hobsworf will find ample opportunity to exercise his obstructive powers, above all in the public sector where the Hobsworf mentality is raised to the status of a way of life. It is no accident that the two examples above come from the British public sector, where outcome-based performance and the discipline of cost-effectiveness can easily be placed second to the office-holder's need to satisfy his Super Ego. Here the bureaucratic personality dominates the style of office-holders' behaviour to the extent that it comes to represent the dominant cultural style and becomes an end in itself.

Personal Experience Exercise

$ Can you identify someone you know who seems to enjoy the status he or she gains from being able to use the 'rules' to wield power over other people?

$ Do you recognise the two case examples from your own experiences? Do the organisations you know have 'professionals' in them who bring their rules with them from outside the organisation?

$ Have you ever encountered the 'm'job's worth' mentality when dealing with office-holders?

CAREERS

Organisations will set obstacles that prevent you from getting potential rewards. They may be saturated with so many rules, and with willing guardians of those rules, as to make them only partially effective at their jobs. Nevertheless you, in common with all others who populate the organisation's offices, need them for what they can provide—a living, security and an outlet for the creative drives that lurk within us all. Your needs provide the source of power that organisations wield over their members and make office-holders behave in a way that will protect their own interests.

Consider the following examples of a manager who was used by the organisation and another who used the organisation for his own ends.

Graphic designer employed by a local newspaper whose readership numbers are dwindling rapidly

1 As a young man he refused to take an art school degree that would have given him generalist, transferable skills.
2 He took a lowly paid apprenticeship in the newspaper with the aim of going up the ladder. He then spent the next twenty years plodding away.
3 Throughout this time he remained committed to the organisation and maintained constant loyalty.
4 He made it to manager (eventually).
5 The arrival of new technology in recent years made his specialist background irrelevant.
6 The company was taken over a few years ago and switched to new technology.
7 A 20-year-old with a two-week course in computer graphics and desk-top publishing can do his job.
8 There is no place for him in bureaucracy.

RESULT: Loser

Distribution manager for a stationery company

1 He sees the organisation as a place to learn skills that are transferable inside and outside the organisation.
2 He uses the organisation to gain training and experience; he attends courses on information technology, inventory control and marketing.
3 With his training behind him, he makes himself useful to other parts of the bureaucracy.
4 He has amassed a set of transferable skills that enable him to switch organisations.
5 He remains with the distribution company only while it offers him advantages.
6 A few years later he takes his experience to organisations where he gets the best price.
7 He uses his experience as a bargaining tool for better jobs.

RESULT: Winner

RIGIDLY BUREAUCRATIC ORGANISATIONS

In describing the characteristics that typified modern bureaucratic organisations, Max Weber drew attention to the dependence of the office-holder on the organisation for a career. Offices are held on to and individuals are promoted up the hierarchy only to the extent that they act and behave in a manner consistent with the rules of the organisation and its offices. Those who are likely to rock the boat are excluded by elaborate selection procedures that keep them out of the organisation in the first place or prevent them from moving up the managerial hierarchy once in.[11] One of the early facts of managerial life that individuals must learn is the need to 'keep one's nose clean'—that is, to avoid taking risks that might lead to adverse comment from those higher in the hierarchy, who have control over the individual's career. Career aspirations and indeed personal survival will be central to the goals of most office-holders. It follows, therefore, that 'risk adverse' behaviour will be a common approach to action in the organisation game. When success at contributing to the overall job of the organisation conflicts with potential career safety, managers will go for the career-safe option at the expense of managerial effectiveness. This tendency is dramatically illustrated by the following example.

During the last war Arthur Davis was invited by the US Navy to study the behaviour of American air crews engaged in anti-submarine warfare in the Pacific.[12] The task of the airborne hunter killers was to identify Japanese submarine targets and then engage them. The battle area of the Pacific was marked out into segments and each air crew was given a carefully worked out patrol schedule that was designed to optimise the number of enemy submarines destroyed. Deviation from the laid-down flight paths was strongly discouraged by superior commanders. The study revealed that a large number of potential 'kills' was being missed and that enemy submarines were slipping through the net designed to catch them. The problem was that whales look very similar to submarines when viewed from the air on the radar screen—a fact that many of these poor creatures learned to their cost during the Falklands conflict in the South Atlantic. Time and time again, career-orientated air crew commanders were found to be ignoring highly likely potential targets that lay just outside their sector. While the extra kill might have contributed to the American war effort, the outside chance that the target was really a whale would have led to a difficult interview with a superior officer to explain that deviation from course on return to base. 'M'job's worth' and careerists following the safe and easy option saved a lot of Japanese submariners from a watery grave in the Pacific.

Personal Experience Exercise

$ Have you ever watched someone in your organisation miss an opportunity to be more effective because the risks of failure might be held against him?

$ Have you missed an opportunity to do a better job for fear that you might 'get it in the neck' for going just outside what somebody in charge might see as 'the rules'?

Professor Laurence Peter, in his famous study of careerism, *The Peter Principle*,[13] pointed out how the hierarchical organisation has an in-built tendency to end up being run by 'yesterday's men'. According to the Peter Principle, those who have proved themselves competent at lower levels in the organisation's hierarchy are promoted to higher office. Eventually, the point is reached where the office-holder is promoted to a 'level of incompetency'. People who may have been excellent junior managers move onwards and upwards to middle executive positions where they are less effective but can still do the job well enough to gain recommendations for promotion. Eventually, however, they will be promoted to a senior post that is beyond their abilities and so organisations end up being run by incompetents.

Reality is worse than Professor Peter's picture would have you believe. Not only are Peter's promoted incompetents often largely unsuited to their higher positions in the organisation, they also bring with them the baggage of their learning picked up on the lower rungs of the hierarchy. Behaviour that stood them in good stead in their earlier careers has brought them success in the past, and therefore they turn to this successful behaviour for a guide to action in their new, higher offices. However, the requirements of higher offices are different, demanding new sets of behaviour and thinking which include leadership, creative thought, decisiveness and even the willingness to take risks to get the job done. The nature of promotion is such that it is just these qualities that will usually have been 'trained out' of managers during their time as junior office-holders. Rather than these higher managerial skills, the senior office-holder will bring with him from his earlier years that set of imperatives that values getting on and getting by through the strategy of keeping his nose clean.

A sad but common sight in organisations is the recently appointed senior manager out of his depth in his new job. Anxious to make his mark and justify his promotion, he busily looks around to find out what he can do. Ironically, he is more adept and comfortable when performing the jobs of his subordinates. He thus clutches at these like straws and proceeds to interfere with the work of those below him in the hierarchy, duplicating effort on lower level tasks while missing more important opportunities for the organisation that would come if he invested his energies in his own job. Worse than the duplication of effort is the effect that this has upon junior office-holders. At best, their scope to use their initiative and creativity will be stunted by the unnecessarily close attentions of the boss who wants to do their jobs for them. At worst, they will become alienated and cease to want to give of their best.

As if all this were not enough, the senior office-holder's problem is exacerbated by the changes in work practices that have taken place since his time of learning in the lower ranks. Few organisations can manage to survive and prosper by doing what they have always done. Adherence to the lessons of past successes is usually a recipe for failure in a world where things are constantly changing and the needs of the present environment are rarely met by the application of past solutions. This truth has never been more self-evident than now, when massive changes in technology have meant that the scope of what organisations can do and the way that they can do them has been altered out of all recognition within a decade rather than a lifetime. The structure of bureaucratic organisations is not, however, geared to the fact that those who are promoted to senior offices will, of necessity, bring with them the lessons and learning of their past.

The senior office-holder is likely to be 'yesterday's man' in another sense. His Super Ego will be rooted in yesterday's ways of doing the organisation's business, which he will impose upon 'today's people' even though they may have a clearer understanding of the present challenges that the organisation faces. This last point deserves illustration. I once watched a senior manager of a very large computer bureau insist upon imposing the rules relating to the testing of a suite of programs, rules that had been drummed into him as a young programmer working on the old massive main frame computers. In the meantime technology had changed and the costly and time-consuming procedures of old had become irrelevant in the world of the modern microcomputer. He was the boss and therefore 'knew best'. He of course imposed his will. The project was delayed but his Super Ego was satisfied.

Personal Experience Exercise

$ Can you identify managers at the top of your organisation who may have been good at lower level jobs but have been promoted out of their depth?

$ Are your superiors decisive risk-takers or do they prefer to play safe?

$ Have you ever felt that your boss spent too much time trying to tell you how to do your job?

> $ Can you think of examples in your own organisation
>   where senior managers have made wrong decisions
>   because they are out of touch with the facts as they
>   are today?

ORGANISATIONAL POLITICS

One of the major problems the winning manager faces is
that, all through our socialisation, our Super Egos have been
indoctrinated by the notion that we as individuals should be
prepared to sacrifice our own selfish wants and desires for
the good of others.[14] The nature of our society is such that
the main outlet for this powerful and primitive human drive
is through attachment to the organisations in which we find
ourselves—first our school and then the organisations from
which we draw our means of livelihood. It has been the
purpose of this chapter to point out how misplaced such
loyalty is.

From your own experience of organisations you will
realise how powerless you are as an individual up against
the seemingly infinite power of the organisation's apparent
ability to control your life and to demand your compliance
by withholding even the basics that you need to survive.
You will know that the common feeling of members of
organisations is alienation—which Robert Blauner defines
as the emotions of 'powerlessness, meaninglessness, isolation
and self estrangement'.[15] I translate this as 'being pissed off'
with having other people run your life for you. The manner
may be impersonal and without malice, but the result is the
same. Because of their nature, organisations are inimical to
your very existence as an individual.

This is not a call to you to make open rebellion. On the
contrary. I have already stressed the need to pay lip-service
to the organisation and its rules—indeed you must learn to
show yourself publicly as an avid supporter of them. Meanwhile find ways of following your own winning agenda that
seem to support the notions of effectiveness that the incompetents above you are likely to value in their terms, and

learn how to manipulate the organisation in order to make it work for your ends by playing the game of organisational politics.

The aim of this strategy is to achieve personal power for the individual rather than the organisation. The advantages can range from the petty (a space in the executive car park, or the size of your office) to the significant (obtaining promotion ahead of the competition). You would be foolish to ignore organisational politics for it exists in almost all organisations. More importantly, you need to be aware of what others are doing around you. The victims of expert politicians usually don't discover they have been screwed until the damage has been done.

How, then, can you ensure that you are not the victim of politicians? By playing them at their own game, of course. Here are just some of the guidelines which winning managers accept as a way of life.

Get yourself noticed

Many of the losers in organisations are the shrinking violets who fail to attract the attention of those in power and authority. They may do a good job, but the people who matter are unaware of this. Keep others informed of your work through progress reports certainly, but more importantly look out for any means of creating and sustaining your positive image in the eyes of your superiors. Although progress reports should be concise, they should contain the essential information: your achievements. Attend company social functions, no matter how boring. Cultivate powerful allies who can be used to support you in promotion applications or proposed projects. Avoid, however, boastfulness and conceit and always remain cool in argumentative situations.

Presentation of self is vital

Always respect the culture of organisations. Culture denotes a set of norms that organisation members are expected to observe. Adherence to them shows that you are a good and (outwardly) loyal organisation member. 'Insider' patterns of behaviour may camouflage the rebel. Failure to conform can result in poor promotion prospects or even the loss of a job.

Although criteria on these matters are seldom written down, culture can easily be adopted by fitting in with the standard way of dress, way to talk to people and the importance placed on the appropriate degree of initiative in a risk-taking situation. But remember to take your cues, not from your peers whose opinion of you does not matter, but rather from your superiors. It is into their culture that you must seem to fit. Winning managers have the chameleon-like ability to fit in and avoid challenging the values of those who already hold power in the organisation. The needs, wants and values of those who do not hold power are irrelevant; ignore them.

Use flattery (even with your opponents)
In addition to creating good will, flattery can sometimes be used to obtain favours from opponents. If, for example, your opponent has rejected your idea for an important new project, defer to his superior knowledge and let him know that you are doing so. This will boost his morale and increase the chance that he will reconsider your idea or at least be more receptive to future ideas. Always remember that only losers refuse to eat humble pie.

Get yourself the support of a patron
This is someone senior to you on the organisational cross, who is respected, experienced and no longer has the need to 'play' politics at your level. He can offer sound advice and can support your progress. Potential rivals might also be reluctant to challenge you if you have a powerful ally. Remember, however, that your chances of obtaining a patron are slim if you do not get noticed as he has to choose you rather than the reverse. He will only support you if you take positive steps to ensure that you are noticed for the right reasons.

Whatever you do, be supportive of your boss
Even though you may fantasise about sticking electrodes up your boss's back package, you have to support him and help him succeed for it is he who controls your immediate future. Other politicians will be only too eager to pick up any disparaging remarks you make about him and carry them back. If your boss gets promoted, he is more likely to take you up with him if you have been supportive. If, however, he is generally regarded as weak, avoid challenging him. Instead, apply for a transfer on the grounds that your talents would be more suited to another area. Never appear disloyal. After all, your boss may not be as stupid as you had thought; he may have cultivated a powerful ally higher up in the organisation . . .

Acquire a group of protégés
Just as you need a patron, so do others below you in the organisational hierarchy. This can provide both parties with an excellent deal. You offer them advice, support and as much help as you can for their ascent up the organisational ladder. In return they watch your back. They support your reputation, but, more importantly, they bring you the intelligence from down below that you need to stay ahead of the opposition. You never know—one of them may be promoted above you and the roles reversed. Either way, you cannot lose.

5 The Winning Agenda

As a winning manager your distinguishing characteristic is that your workplace agenda is subordinate to your aim of gaining power for yourself. Remember, this does not always mean what is conventionally thought of as holding power: it means being in control of your destiny. It means deciding what you want and then ensuring that you achieve this on your terms rather than other people's. While some may strive for the title of Managing Director and the wealth and status attached to it, others may desire the power to influence decisions, the power to do their job in the way they want or perhaps even the power to resist the power of others in the organisation.

It follows from this that you must have a good idea of what you want. If you are not to become prey to the usual loser's recipe of falling in with what others around you are doing, then you must take the time and trouble to work out clearly how you are going to control your environment. You need to begin your winning manager's career by establishing a clear picture of what you want from the system.

Defining your aim in terms of the way that it will help you to gain control over your life is, however, not an end in itself. Aims are useless to you unless you make them your guiding principles. You must make the aim of gaining control of your life central to all your actions in the organisation. From now on, everything you do as a manager must be judged in terms, not of how it pleases the Super Egos of those about you, but how far it contributes to your pursuit of power. This must be your only criterion for taking action.

The decision to pursue and obtain power in the organisation is vital. Without it, you will be subject to the definitions of others as to how you should conduct yourself in your day-to-day actions. The various groups that seek to influence your behaviour will pull you in the direction of doing what they want you to do for their ends. The organisation itself will draw you into doing what every good organisational member has always done.

This weapon of knowledge of what you want from the organisation is particularly powerful because it will not be available to your enemies. The losers who surround you will not have made this choice. They are too stupid, too scared, too cowed or too constrained by their fear of their own Super Egos. This places you in a strong position in your dealings with them. In place of the loser's reaction to the imperatives of managerial life, you can become proactive; you will have taken a major step towards becoming a winner.

Perhaps one of the best examples of a winner was Vladimir Illich Lenin. While others contented themselves with the abstractions of political philosophy, he started with a clear idea of what had to be done.[1] Love him or loathe him, he set out to change the world and, with singlemindedness and dedication, he did just what he said he would. But his success in the 'doing' came from knowing first what he wanted to do. Like all successful people, he had a vision, not only of how he had to go about the business of winning, but what he wanted to achieve. He had a clear set of goals which he then pursued relentlessly.

If you look for confirmation of the need to be clear about your goals, listen to what that prophet of managerial effectiveness, Peter Drucker, has to say on the subject. In his book *The Effective Executive*,[2] he shows that the absence of clearly defined managerial goals against which to base action leads to a proliferation of conflicting ideas about what has to be done. Drucker sees this as a recipe for organisational failure. He draws a vivid example from the British nationalised airlines British European Airways (BEA) and the British Overseas Airways Corporation (BOAC), both of which faced corporate collapse before they were rescued in the massive restructuring of the Sixties.

These airlines seemed to operate with no sense of purpose.

Drucker lists four goals that were to be found in their Web-
erian 'collective memory'—profit, service to the customer,
support for the UK aerospace industry and the maintenance
of a British presence on the tarmac of airports around the
world. Drucker's point is that these goals were mutually
incompatible. Because the managers of these organisations
did not make an attempt to question what business they
were in, to question their goals, they followed a typical
'common sense' approach of 'we all know what we should
be doing, don't we?' The result was organisational disaster.
For the details read Drucker's book, but let me highlight
two problems from BOAC's ill-considered approach to its
existence. From the days of a British Empire on which 'the
sun never set', it saw its duty as providing an airline service
to all parts of the Commonwealth. The fact that few people
wanted to travel on most of these links meant that the airline
continued to divert aeroplanes from money-making non-
Commonwealth runs to the detriment of both profitability
and service to the customer.

The goal of support for Britain's aircraft industry led
to BOAC's decision to buy the British-made de Havilland
Comet, the world's first jet airliner. In its early years the
aeroplane was a commercial failure: its propensity to
develop cracks and to crash cost the company vast sums
of money in inspection, maintenance and grounded flights.
Nevertheless, BOAC continued to buy the Comet. A company really concerned with profit or service to the customer
would have ditched this costly and dangerous British liability
and bought the American Boeing Strato-Cruiser.

Drucker's account of the failure of the British nationalised
airlines uncovers another set of goals followed by the managers who ran them. Like a lot of industries, the airline
business has a culture of its own. The Second World War
exposed a lot of people to what they saw as the magic of
flying. When hostilities ceased, they naturally joined the
newly burgeoning airlines such as BEA and BOAC. But
they did so not because they cared about service to the
customer or about helping these companies make a profit,
it was love of the culture of the airways that drove them.

When these people were promoted into management posts they continued to be obsessed by their love of flying and neglected the tasks of running the airlines. As a result, they were directed more by the culture of the industry than by the need to make the airlines a commercial and operational success.

Drucker could equally have picked on other examples where mixed and unclear managerial goals have had disastrous effects. Only in the last ten years has the British coal industry woken up to the need to be profitable.[3] The joke about British Rail—an enterprise run by train-spotters for the National Union of Railwaymen—is only just beginning to lose its point since the appointment of an experienced, hard-nosed businessman, Sir Bob Reid, to take control. Drucker's lessons from the government-owned British airlines are even more true for you as an individual.

The business of achieving power in an organisation is like a physical journey. From the moment you arrive there you begin a journey that leads you to a destination—a position in the organisation's hierarchy of offices. Only a fool would set out on a physical journey without first deciding where he intended to end up. Only a loser would set out on an organisational journey, trusting to the winds and the tides of managerial life to dictate the final destination. The winning manager is one who takes this analogy seriously and follows a similar approach.

Personal Experience Exercise
$ Can you identify someone in your organisation who clearly knows what he wants and sets out to get it?
$ Is there someone else who seems to have no idea what he wants and is driven by the whim of the moment?
$ Ask yourself where you want to be in the organisation in five years' time. Be honest, do you have an answer?

PLANNING

Think about making a physical journey. Think how you would work out your destination first and then go about the business of getting there. You will see how the same approach to your organisational journey will give you a head start. Staying with the physical journey, let me give you an example from my own experience, of moving from Oxford in England to take up a new job in Glasgow. The map looks like this:

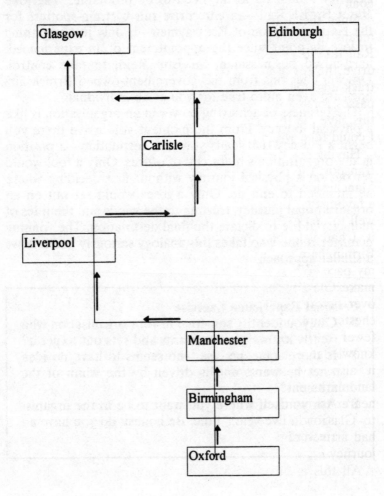

Like any sensible traveller, I had already decided where I was to go. In my heart the journey back to Scotland was coloured by the pull of familiar, stylish, cosmopolitan Edinburgh—the Athens of the North—with its smart capital city self-confidence. Ahead of me, however, was my chosen destination—industrial Glasgow. I wished I was going East but no amount of wishful thinking was going to help me in reaching the destination where my job took me. My eyes had to be focused westwards and towards my goal.

Once the destination was clear I could think about the means of getting there. Should I fly? Should I let British Rail take me, with a change at Birmingham? Or should I drive the seven-hour flog up the muddled mixture of cart track upgraded to main road and crumbling motorways that passes for a road system in Britain? I decided to drive as this gave me the freedom to choose the amount of luggage I could take with me.

Having made the decision as to destination and mode of transport the next step was to plan the route: Birmingham, Manchester, Carlisle and Scotland. In doing so I did myself a favour that the winner in the organisation game would do well to mark. By knowing my destination and the route to it, I had valuable information for action. When I reached Birmingham earlier than I had expected I was able to slow my pace. When I hit Manchester late, I knew I would not make Glasgow in daylight and made the decision to stop over before the border. When I missed my way at Manchester and began to see the miles to Liverpool getting fewer on the signposts, I knew I was off my course. All this knowledge provided me with vital material for action, but it also gave me reward and encouragement. As the landmarks passed by, I could see I was getting nearer and nearer to my destination. When I passed the first turn-off to Glasgow, I knew that my journey was nearly over. I had arrived and could begin to concentrate upon my next journey.

All this is obvious to anyone contemplating a physical

journey. But how many managers take the trouble to think out their destination, the means of getting there and the route they must take in their journeys through organisational life? If you think about it, the same needs for knowledge-based decision-making and for satisfaction and encouragement apply. The alternative is to do the equivalent of pointing the motor car at Scotland and driving hell for leather in the hope of getting there sometime. Yet this is what most managers do when faced with the journey through the organisation.

Although the need to plan should be obvious, a recurrent theme I find when talking to managers about the need to set goals and to plan is the idea that there is just no time for these vital activities. In the bustle to get things done, planning what you want to do and where you want to go is a vital ingredient of success. All the knowledge of the constraints that hold you back from gaining power is of little value unless you use it for planning how to win the organisation game.

Alec MacKenzie, in his two excellent books on time management, *The Time Trap*[4] and *Managing Time at the Top*,[5] demonstrates the importance of planning through the results of a study that compared the workings of two sets of company projects. One set was undertaken with an approach that emphasised the need for managers to spend time on planning. Another, similar set was carried out with managers under the usual pressure to get involved quickly in action for execution of their projects. His findings show the superiority of the planning approach over the unthinking drive to immediate action. A typical 'planning culture' project was shown to have about twice as much time devoted to its planning stage as a project in the 'action'-orientated environment. Despite this longer planning period, during which nothing seemed to be done, the projects of the planning culture were regularly completed in a shorter time, typically around 87 per cent of the time taken by their action-orientated counterparts. While the action-based approach seemed to get things moving quickly, the planning approach avoided subsequent hitches and delays by eliminating more of the avoidable difficulties before they escalated. Moreover, the planned projects were not only more successful in terms of the speed of their implementation, they were found to produce better commercial results and were judged by managers to be qualitatively better all round.

A problem you face is that you will have been brought up in a managerial environment that has taught you a set of Super Ego 'rules' that equate immediate action with success. The image of the winning manager that pervades our culture is one of the 'action man' who tackles problems head on with the minimum of delay. There is little room in this vision for the notion of standing back and making a considered approach to problems. Changing the culture of the organisation and making it a more effective vehicle for your ambitions is not an easy task. A lone manager crying out for more time and effort to be spent on planning is unlikely to get the sympathetic hearing of superiors who have been brought up in a culture of action.

Two strategies are, however, open to you. Firstly, in the areas where you are responsible for results, you need to develop an atmosphere in which time and trouble spent on planning are seen to be time well spent. In this you will have to educate your subordinates who will also be used to working to the rule that action rather than thinking produces results. More importantly, you must work on yourself. You will only win the organisation game through action that is conceived as part of a plan, and by injecting an ethic of planning into all that you do you will enhance your image as someone who obtains successful outcomes for the organisation. But the real winning manager's agenda—ensuring that everything you do is calculated to serve your own interests— also requires time for thinking and planning.

You may wish that you could find the time to control your managerial life and become proactive rather than having to react to everyday pressures. A frequent complaint among managers, however, is that they just do not seem to have any breathing space at all in their busy schedule. This is an excuse that losers often use to justify their failure to take a hold of their managerial lives. The simple answer is that there exist whole pieces of time in your everyday routine, which you could use for planning but which are wasted. This is not a book on time management. If you want a detailed programme for regaining control of your time, read Mac-Kenzie's *The Time Trap* which I have already cited. Suffice to say that between twenty and thirty minutes a day should be enough for most managers to plan the control of their managerial lives, once they have got themselves into a routine based upon a planning system. Because your brain is a parallel processor,[6] it can carry on with one activity when interrupted to engage upon another. It therefore does not matter if these twenty or thirty minutes are made up of small three- or five-minute periods spread over the day. In fact, spacing them out makes them more effective. While you are consciously occupied in thinking of something else, another part of your brain will carry on where you left off in your planning process. Setting up such a system will take you as little as an hour once you have finished reading this book.

Personal Experience Exercise

$ Can you think of a time when the pressure to get things done has led you to leap into a project without having had a chance to think it through properly?

$ How do you occupy your mind when travelling to work? How long is your journey? What do you think about?

$ How do you spend your time waiting for an appointment that is delayed?

WHERE DO YOU WANT TO GO?

There are two facts about power that are not immediately apparent to those seeking it. The first is that absolute power does not exist in organisations: even the most despotic senior manager is severely limited in what he can or cannot do.

The constraints come not merely from such things as legal or economic issues, but are part of the political realities of organisational life.[7] If you look at the life-style of people at the top, they often seem to be driven by the same set of external controlling forces that are the source of alienation and frustration to those farther down the hierarchy. A high-ranking post in the management structure is unlikely to be a satisfying source of power.

The second reality is that the management pyramid narrows sharply. There are few places at the top and there are many managers struggling to achieve them. Further, due to the promotion process, the avenues to the top are closed to many who embark on the wrong career path.[8]

You should therefore look elsewhere than mere hierarchical promotion for means of achieving power in the organisation. A far more realistic goal is to seek to gain power not by the attainment of office alone, but by the pursuit of influence.[9] Few managers can control their lives by the direct exercise of imposing their will upon events and upon others. However, at all levels in organisations, there exist opportunities for you to influence the decisions that affect your life.

The power of influence that attaches to offices cannot be measured by their rank in the formal hierarchy. For example, the influence exerted by the chief executive's secretary is greater than that of most board members. Throughout any organisation there are offices that are pivotal to the process of influencing decision-makers and they are where the real power lies. It thus follows that you should ignore the quest for formal status alone; instead, you must identify those offices that can bring influence to bear on the people who make the decisions. You can then set about gaining the closest possible proximity to the ears and minds of the office-holders who control life in the organisation, or consider targeting those positions for yourself.

When he worked at San Marcos College (later Southwestern Texas State Teachers College) Lyndon Johnson was determined to cultivate the friendship and respect of some of the most influential people who would help him climb the San Marcos hierarchy. One of the most important men he identified was Cecil Evans, President of the College, who was highly influential among the faculty and student body. Johnson succeeded in being appointed special assistant to the president's personal secretary.

His duties in this role were simply to carry messages from the president to the department heads and other faculty members. Johnson, however, realised that this post had potential. He began to encourage recipients of the messages to transmit their own messages through him. He occupied a desk in the president's outer office where he announced the arrival of visitors. The added services eventually became so important that faculty members regarded Johnson as a channel to the president. By applying the same technique which would later enable him to control Congress, Johnson turned a rather menial service into a process through which power was exercised.

Evans, recognising Johnson's abilities, made him responsible for handling his political correspondence and preparing his reports for state agencies with jurisdiction over the college and its funding. Johnson was quick to point out that he was familiar with the workings of the legislature and the personalities of its leaders through accompanying his father, who had been a member of the state legislature (from 1905 to 1909 and from 1918 to 1925), to a number of meetings. Soon he began to accompany Evans on his trips to the state capital in Austin and become a reliable source of political advice. Johnson was a natural 'political' animal, a slick performer whether sitting in a committee room or standing on the floor talking to representatives. His reports to Evans were noted for their accuracy and entertainment value. The older man, on whose favour Johnson depended, now relied on him as an invaluable source of advice.[10]

Pick a date in the future, say ten years from now. Imagine that all the breaks have gone your way. With the aim of achieving power in the organisation through influence, ask yourself what job *should* you be doing? What are your areas of responsibility? What access to decision-making does the job give you? What access does the job give you to those who make the decisions that control your life in the organisation?

The answers to these questions are the equivalent of choosing a destination for a journey. If you have answered them honestly and realistically, you now have a goal that you can set in front of you, by which you can guide your direction in everyday life. Having decided where you want to go, you can judge every action you make or are required to make in terms of how far it might contribute to your arrival at that destination on time. The route will not be straight or easy, just as travelling on the UK road system is not straight or easy. Sometimes the unexpected will block your way, but you now have a means of judging when to make the necessary detour and how to get back on the track that you have chosen. If you make a detour to oblige the whims of a group of your peers who really have no power to stop you in your journey, or if you take a longer, slower route, merely because that is the way that everybody else travels your sort of organisational journey, the choice is yours. But by having a destination in front of you, you will be able to judge the consequence of such a detour to the achievement of your goal.

Although the above formula may make sense to most managers, the bustle of everyday life will often mean that good intentions, even when written down like New Year's resolutions, will be an easy victim to old habit, expediency or sheer lack of resolve. The whole business of thinking about the future is also daunting—the task is just too big. You may need something to help you start the business of planning your managerial goals, and a clear and effective means of keeping your eye on the goal you have selected for yourself.

The Personal Experience Exercises below are aimed at imprinting the goal that you have set yourself firmly in the mind, so that it will not be pushed aside by the other pressing matters that impinge upon your consciousness. The exercises require you to do more than merely put names to the events of your imagined future. They require you to 'experience' the future, as it could be, with all its sights, sounds, feelings and even smells. Having done this they invite you to turn this experience into a symbol that you can put in front of you like a beacon beckoning you forward towards your goal. Again, you can choose to ignore it, but it will always be there, reminding you that you could decide to be a winner in the organisation game.

Personal Experience Exercise

$ Think again about the job which you are going to make the target of your ambition to achieve power through influence.

$ Do not just say to yourself, 'I want to be the Marketing Manager.' Think of the sights and sounds that will surround you. Imagine the feel of the Marketing Manager's chair and desk! Think of the smell of the leather of the BMW's upholstery!

$ Now take a pencil and construct a personal logo, a quickly sketched little picture that will bring back to you these sights, sounds and feelings whenever you look at it.

Here are three examples of personal logos from the success stories of managers who began their winners' careers with a clear goal in front of them, translated into something that they could visualise now:

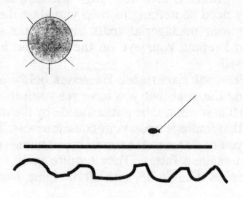

This is from a manager who had a love of fishing, the sun and freedom. He wanted promotion to a job where he would be paid to go to sunny climes and indulge his hobby. He is now a senior sales executive specialising in selling to the leisure market in Spain and the Caribbean.

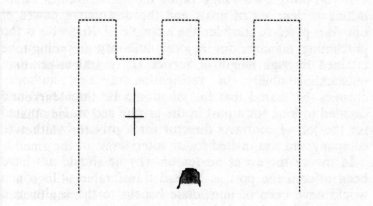

Here is a woman who designed office interiors for a company. She wanted to be 'queen of her own castle' and to design castles, or at least smart houses, without the constraints of commercial functionality. She now has her own business helping people renovate and redecorate old houses.

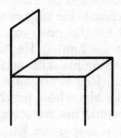

This man left a safe career to start again at the bottom of an academic career. He desperately wanted the autonomy and encouragement to pursue research interests that a professorial chair would bring him. He is now writing this book.

If you think I am exaggerating the importance of establishing a clear set of goals and the destructive power of our own psyches, consider the example of Reg who is the purchasing manager for a local authority, a position he attained through length of service (15 years) rather than outstanding ability. In anticipation of local authority changes, he feared that his job would be threatened and decided to look for a post in the private sector. He applied for the job of contracts director for a private health care company and was invited for an interview.

In theory there was no reason why he should not have been offered the post as he had transferable skills which would have been of immediate benefit to the health care company. These included:

- strong project management skills,
- 'political' awareness of changes in the health sector,
- strong organisational ability,
- a clear sense of cost-effectiveness.

At interview, however, Reg did his best to ensure that he was struck off the short list of candidates. When asked why he felt he would be good at the job he replied that he 'wasn't really sure' and continued by explaining why he might not be their ideal candidate. He suggested, for instance, that he might be too old for the post and that his experience of private health care was limited. He made no attempt to 'sell' himself by emphasising his skills and experience.

Believe it or not, Reg is not an isolated example. There are many losers like him whose psyches have a self-destruct mechanism. Reg would not have been invited to the interview if his potential employers had not believed he could do the job; yet his own psyche had convinced him he was incapable of succeeding. He had no sense of direction in his life, nor any belief in his abilities. Faced with the same situation, a winner would have reacted entirely differently:

- Firstly, he would be convinced that he wanted the job and that he was the right man to do it.
- He would have researched the needs of the health care company and identified ways in which he could satisfy them.
- He would have adopted a confident and positive attitude throughout the interview. Anyone who believes he is a winner is half-way there; read the rest of this book and the other half of your journey is complete.
- Even if he didn't get the job, the winner would treat it as a minor setback rather than a major catastrophe. He would work out what went wrong and try to avoid disappointment the next time. A loser would waste time licking wounds and would be paralysed from trying again through fear of failure.

Take your personal logo and put it in places where you cannot ignore its presence. Put it above your make-up mirror or your shaving glass so that it nags at you every morning. Place it on your desk, so that when you are dealing with the losers who inhabit your world, you can remind yourself that you are not going to dwell amongst them for much longer. Make sure that it is the first thing that you see when you open your personal organiser.[11] When you have finished reading this chapter your personal organiser will be full of things that you have to do. You will need a constant reminder of why you have to do them if you want to sustain the momentum of being a winner.

ROUTES AND OBSTACLES

In this chapter I have shown you how to draw a map of your journey through the organisation to attain your goal. The description of a way in which the geography of organisations is structured identifies what lies between you and the achievement of your future. You will now be able to see where your vision lies in terms of the hierarchy of managerial offices that lie on your route. You will also be able to work out which offices control the route and the organisational rules that govern their operation.

Just as anyone planning a physical journey should have a clear picture of the route to his destination, so you need to draw up an organisational 'route card' with a clear idea of the office that you intend to attain as its destination. Working back from this, you will be able to see what offices you will need to have held in order to reach your destination. This will allow you to identify the current holders of those offices and to discover how they came to occupy them. You can then see what qualifications, skills and attributes for promotability got others selected for the offices that you will need to occupy and which could do the same for you.

The potential obstacles that could hinder your progress lie within your own psyche. As we saw in Chapter Two, people are their own worst enemies. Each of us carries within us the seeds of our own failure in the form of a loser's mentality. We may want to be winners on one level, but our sense of conformity, our fears about what others might think and our own treacherous Super Egos have taught us to set other priorities. The first stage of identifying obstacles to winning is, therefore, to look within yourself to find the barriers that your inner self has put in front of you. Ask yourself what loyalties or friendships you value more than the achievement of your goal, and what conventional rules you would not be prepared to break in order to succeed.

This is usually a difficult and painful task; it is much easier to assess what you lack in terms of knowledge and abilities. You should examine your skills and see if they match those required for your planned destination. You will almost certainly need to show that you have successfully held down junior offices before you can be trusted with more senior positions. There may be sideways moves in the hierarchy that will provide useful experience, such as a spell working with computers or learning how to handle personnel problems. There will be training courses that will teach you useful skills and demonstrate your determination to fit yourself for advancement. There may even be special projects for which you can volunteer in order to gain additional experience and the reputation for having it. Only you can judge what these skills and types of experience should be. The time to consider them, however, is when you are planning your route to your goal, not retrospectively after you have been turned down for promotion because of their lack or because you have wasted your time in acquiring the wrong skills and the wrong experience. You should think in terms of building up a curriculum vitae that will act as a passport to your vision of your future.

Personal Experience Exercise

$ What offices lie between you and your aim? Draw a 'route card' of offices, starting with where you are now and ending with where you want to be.

$ Who are the managers who occupy these offices? Put names to the various offices on the route.

$ How did they get where they are? What qualifications, skills and attributes for promotion did they have?

MAKING YOUR AGENDA WORK

Once you are clear about where you want to go and what might stand in your way, you must concentrate whole-heartedly upon the means of getting there. The aim of the remainder of this chapter is to offer you a way of setting about turning the vision of your future into practical action.

While you must concentrate on fitting yourself to hold future offices in your organisation, being suited for promotion to senior management is not a sufficient guarantee that it will materialise. Indeed, as Norman Dixon shows in relation to military hierarchies,[12] some characteristics that are valued in senior organisational members, such as initiative and independence of mind, are a hindrance to the preferment of junior personnel where these characteristics may be seen as evidence of inability to fit in to the disciplined structure of the organisation. Albeit with sights set firmly on the future, you need to examine the here and now for the basis on which to build success.

Your success as a manager relies upon your ability to shift product. Your job will have a number of key sectors that are vital for success, and you must be able to identify these and concentrate upon them. You will also be beset by a whole host of 'crap' jobs, some of which will have been inherited from your predecessor, while others will have been foisted on you by your Super Ego with its misguided notion that you are in the organisation for some reason other than to achieve your own ends. You need a method of deciding what will help you to advance and what is a waste of your time, energies and concentration. The former must be the focus of all your managerial effort; the latter you should discard, as you might when packing a travelling bag to conform to an airline baggage allowance.

Personal Experience Exercise

$ Think of an example of something you do that is vital to your pay packet, your promotion chances or the good will of your superiors.

$ Can you also think of something that you do as part of your job, but which seems to contribute nothing? What would happen if this job did not get done? Would anyone who matters notice or care?

In order to make decisions like this about your entire job, you need to have a clear picture of what factors are central to the work you do. The criterion for judging centrality, however, must not be the traditional one that we have already seen is likely to have been foisted on you by someone else's vision of the world; it must be based solely upon your vision and what you have to do to achieve it.

Your key sectors will form the basis for planning action. The list must consist of no less than six and no more than eight headings. Fewer than six means that you have failed to identify all the stages for completing the journey towards your goal. More than eight, so the psychologists tell us,[13] will be difficult to hold in the mind as an overview. It is vital that you do not overlook any key sector.

As this approach is a purely practical one, it needs a practical example. Every manager's job is different, but I have chosen to take my example from the field that I know best—academic management. When it comes to your turn to do the exercise for yourself you will, of course, have a very different set of headings. My example highlights seven key sectors that a university lecturer, a junior academic manager, should develop as his guide to action if his goal is to be appointed to a professorial chair.

TEACHING
ACADEMIC ADMINISTRATION
RESEARCH
PUBLICATION
FUNDING ACTIVITIES
SELF-DEVELOPMENT
PUBLIC RELATIONS

The rationale for each of the key sectors might be as follows:

TEACHING: This is central to your current job and your vision. You must be seen to do it well and be fully conversant with the latest teaching methods.

ACADEMIC ADMINISTRATION: Can you develop and run new courses? Can you manage existing ones? This is a key indicator of suitability for promotion to a senior management position.

RESEARCH: Professorial chairs go to academics who produce good research. You cannot ignore the need to involve yourself in research projects.

PUBLICATION: Research quality is measured by the number of acknowledgements it receives in learned journals.

FUNDING ACTIVITIES: Modern universities need to attract

funds from a variety of sources. To be suitable for a senior post, you must show you can bring in research grants.

SELF-DEVELOPMENT: What skills are you lacking to do your current job well? What can you do to be seen to fit yourself for promotion?

PUBLIC RELATIONS: Being good at the above things is only half the battle. Whom do you have to convince that you are good in order to gain the appropriate recognition? How can you bring yourself to their attention? Who and what might get in the way of a 'good' reputation?

If you take time to think about the key sectors that are relevant to your career path through the organisation, then you will see that the result provides a clear set of rules for action. First, the list will remind you where you have to look for projects that will help you to achieve your vision—what projects help you to shift product. Second, and just as importantly, it will help you to identify the projects on which you should *not* waste time. If a new opportunity arises but does not fit into your list, avoid it. If it is forced on you, apply the minimum degree of time and effort and save your energies for your own ambitions.

Your list of key sectors will also help you identify behaviour in which you should never engage if you want to reach your vision as quickly as possible. Again, I take an example from academia. One of the facts about academic life is that one is surrounded by a host of young people many of whom are experimenting with their own sexuality for the first time. The older man or woman could have a sexual field day in this environment. In academic institutions this is called 'Gross Moral Turpitude' (GMT) and is usually a disciplinary offence. My advice to the owner of the above set of key sector headings is to avoid the temptation of GMT as inimical to your success in gaining power in the organisation. If it does not get you the sack, it will at least be counterproductive to your efforts in the sector of PUBLIC RELATIONS. If you happen to be an academic and your vision is one of libidinous indulgence, however ... But then you would have identified a different set of key sectors.

Personal Experience Exercise
$ List at least six key sectors that are vital to your job and which will contribute to your attaining your vision.
$ Why are these important?

Having completed your list, you need to ensure that it is incorporated into action to help you achieve your aim. It must be constantly in your view so that you have no excuse for 'forgetting' to put your energies into sectors that you have decided are important but which are difficult or troublesome. Nothing on the list must be allowed to escape your attention. You must therefore place your list of key sectors, written in pencil so that you can delete or add items as circumstances change, at the front of your personal organiser opposite your personal logo, so that it cannot escape your notice. Every time you open it up you will be presented with an overview of the areas where you must devote your energies if you are to achieve your aim of gaining power in the organisation. Open up a section for each heading so that you can include all the notes relating to one key sector in one place.

Because your managerial life will be dynamic and things that are relevant today may not be useful to you in the future, you need to review your key sectors regularly. Once a week, during one of the slots of otherwise wasted time that you have identified, look at the list carefully. Ask yourself what you have done in the past week to make each of the key sectors work towards your vision. Once a month, in a similarly regained time slot, review the list. Decide if the headings are still those that will help you on your journey. Have any ceased to be relevant? Are there new key sectors that could serve your vision any better?

ACTION TO WIN

Your aim is to become proactive: rather than be a creature of the organisation, you need to find ways of making the organisation work for you. Having identified the key sectors where your effort will be rewarded, your next step is to turn this knowledge into action that will lead to success in your aim. The key sectors are your means of travelling towards your goal; you now need to find the route.

The list of key sectors gives you a means of deciding what projects you should ignore. What you need to do is find their positive counterpart—those projects that require your involvement if you are to be successful in each of your key sectors.

You need a means of concentrating on what you must do now. Of course, the same rule applies as to Key Sectors—only include projects that will bring you nearer to your vision and help shift product. Try to avoid everything else that the organisation tries to dump on you.

Let us take the example of a man who has to manage a large number of people in a department. He would be well advised to have a key sector of STAFF on his list. What might he include in his list of projects derived from this sector? Using some of the many periods of time that he has found are available to him, he might come up with the following:

TASK IDENTIFICATION: Deciding what tasks will have to be carried out by the department.

RESPONSIBILITY PLANNING: Allocating the assignments to people.

MOTIVATING: Ensuring that the staff are inspired to carry out their jobs to the best of their abilities.

MONITORING: Setting performance indicators and monitoring results.

TRAINING: Deciding on what training will make for a more effective department.

RULES: Establishing the rules of conduct of members of the department.

DEVELOPMENT: Looking at the training and motivational needs of individuals.

RECRUITMENT: Identifying and meeting future staffing needs.

APPRAISAL: Evaluating subordinates' performance and giving feedback.

COUNSELLING: Highlighting positive contributions and bringing underperformers up to the required standard.

As you can see, the breaking down of key sectors into projects allows you to concentrate on discovering exactly what has to be done in order to be successful in areas that you have already decided will contribute to your progress. Try the process for yourself. Examine your own list of key sectors and look for the projects in which you need to get involved. Again, as with your key sectors, one of the major factors in making the system work is your ability to have an overview of what you must do to achieve your aim. As you identify a project, make a separate page for it in the section of your personal organiser devoted to its key sector. Again, this will both keep it firmly to the front of your otherwise crowded mind and allow you to review its contribution to product shifting when you go over your work plan at regular intervals.

What we are aiming at is a translation of your vision of your future in the organisation, through key sectors and projects, into gains that can be achieved here and now to bring that vision nearer to reality. There is therefore one last step in the process – turning the projects into the practical tasks that have to be done—actual assignments.

A winning manager should be a delegator. The system outlined above will, if you use it properly, help you to concentrate upon winning.

Personal Experience Exercise
$ Take one of the pages of your personal organiser headed with the name of a project. Make a list of all the things that have to be done for this project.
$ For each assignment, ask yourself, 'By what date does it have to be completed?'
$ Is the deadline you have set realistic, or is it based

on wishful thinking?

$ Who should do which assignments? Wherever possible, you should look to pass an assignment to someone else on the management cross. A skilled manager will learn to delegate assignments upwards to superiors or sideways to colleagues as well as downwards to subordinates. Only a loser tries to do everything himself

$ Carry out the same exercise for all your projects.

$ At some time every week, review the list of assignments for every project on your lists.

$ Make sure you follow up all the assignments you have delegated to ensure that they have been carried out! Include the assignments you have kept for yourself in the follow-up process.

THE WINNING AGENDA

As we have seen, the secret to being a winning manager is having a clear vision of what you want to get out of the organisation. Once you have made up your mind how you want the organisation to work for you, it becomes possible to arrange the structure of your managerial life according to *your* vision and not that of the other people around you who have agendas that are hostile to you and your needs.

You will have noticed a number of themes running through the ideas that I have presented to you. You will see that winning requires action rather than reaction, proactivity rather than reactivity. It requires you to spend time and energy thinking actively about your place in the organisation and to find the time to plan your route from your present position towards your chosen future. At a mundane and practical level, it requires you to spend time in reviewing your goals and the means appropriate to achieving them. You will also note that I have continually stressed the need to commit the various stages to paper.

One of the problems with people is that they are born liars. And the most frequent victims of the lies are individuals themselves. The emphasis upon documentation – upon urging you to develop a personal logo and a set of written lists—is to force you to be confronted with the choices that you have made for yourself. Then, when faced with the everyday pressure to give in and conform to life in your organisation, you will have the choice of listening to the subverting voices within you telling you, 'It is all too difficult', or you can stick to your agenda and strive to reach your goal.

6 Buying Souls

Managers are very rarely in control of their fate in the
organisation game. The world consists of people who will
constantly try to impose their wishes and definitions on you,
obstructing your chosen path. On the other hand, to perform
as a manager you need people. As we have seen, the very
nature of the job is one of getting things done by and
through others.[1] Quite simply, if you want results, you need
help.

We have already noted that the biggest obstacles to your
domination of the managerial world stem from human
characteristics. The fact that people combine to form groups
makes them powerful. It is meant to do so. The power
that allowed primeval man to dominate his harsh physical
environment also enables modern man to dominate the
organisational environment. And this power is a threat to
you in your aim to impose your will on the organisation.

But you can take heart. Although groups are potentially
strong and threatening, people as individuals are weak. If
you can separate the individuals around you from the influence of others, you can tame them to become subservient
to your ends as a cowboy might herd mustangs and break
them to become domesticated horses. As with the process
of turning a wild creature into a biddable domestic animal,
however, you need cunning and stealth to achieve your ends,
rather than the unthinking, heavy-handed approach that
seems to characterise much of what passes for modern management.

To be a winner, you need to control not only people's
actions—their bodies—but also the mental processes that
lie behind those actions—their souls. Like Mephistopheles,

the legendary earthly agent of the 'Prince of Lies', you must learn how to buy the souls of the people who can help you win. Having done so, you will need to know how to manipulate them to get what you want from them.

Personal Experience Exercise
$ Can you think of someone you manage whose absence from your team would make getting the job done more difficult?
$ Are there people around you whose cooperation you would like to gain?

THE TRIAD GETS IN YOUR WAY

As ever, when pursuing your ambitions, your psyche will try to obstruct you. The need to control and manipulate people for your own ends is a fact of managerial life, the very basis of what management is about, but it conflicts with all the teachings of conventional morality. From early in our social development, we inherit the belief that attempting to manipulate others is unacceptable.

Once you have acknowledged the need to do so, however, you will have no problem—provided you can rid yourself of the usual set of losers' ideas that hold you back: the Triad.[2] Never underestimate the power of these internal enemies. They will have made your managerial capabilities a prisoner of a number of very powerful myths which, if allowed to dominate your actions, will lead you into the ways of the loser.

A common myth that managers fall for is the idea that people cannot be 'bought'. The idealistic wishful thinking of your moralising Super Ego will try to tell you that people protect their personal integrity—their souls—and will not let themselves be subverted from their notions of 'what is right for them' by the offer of reward. So strong will be the propaganda on behalf of this myth that at a conscious level you may actually have come to believe it to be true. On the other hand, just look around you. Everywhere you turn, you will see people doing things that are against their nature, in order to fulfil some objective. You will note, however, that there is always a pay-off: people compromise for a reward.

Much of modern thinking about organisations, after Weber, sees life in them in terms of a 'negotiated order'— as entities built on the compliance of their members by a trade-off of compromises that reflect the realities of the power relations prevalent at any given time. This in itself gives the lie to the notion that people cannot be persuaded to do for reward what they would otherwise not do. Their souls are clearly for sale, in vast quantities, all the time. Mephistopheles, whose most famous purchase was the soul of Dr Faustus, knew this. He merely had to apply himself to finding the right currency and the right price. As with most people, it was not money that bought Faust. But more of this later.

You will almost certainly have been exposed to a loser's morality that argues that, even if people's souls can be bought, they *should* not be. Your Super Ego will also have learnt that it is wrong to manipulate individuals' weaknesses in order to achieve your ends. The choice is yours. But, as we have seen above, by its very definition of 'getting things done by and through other people', the concept of management implies that people are open to persuasion. As a winner you will recognise that everyone's soul has its price and that this knowledge can be turned into power to achieve your ends.

Another myth that will subvert you from your goal stems from the Ego's mistaken idea that the behaviour of people in organisations is always rational and that consequently they will invariably do what you want them to do. They are always open to your reasoned argument and will come to see that they have an interest in cooperating with you to achieve the 'best' possible outcome. This is sheer fallacy. As we have seen, the whole business of action in organis-ations is founded as much upon the inner drives of the Freudian Triad as it is upon rational thinking and evaluation. For example, Ego-style rationality cannot be imputed to people who are subject to the irrational influence of groups, hard though it might be for the Ego and Super Ego to accept this.

The same myth also overlooks the existence of so-called 'multiple rationalities'. People will have different ways of looking at the world about them, based upon different perspectives and experiences. Norman Dixon, for example, shows how incompetent military managers have often brought disaster upon their commands because of their failure to realise that their enemies might not have the same goals and perceptions of the world.[3] An example from the world of geo-politics will clarify this point. Much of Britain's difficulty in her relations with the Arab world stems from the narrow perspectives of one man: former British Prime Minister Anthony Eden. When confronted with the nationalism of Egypt's Colonel Nasser in 1956, Eden could not see beyond the pre-Second World War nationalist, Adolf Hitler. Nationalist leaders, even those like Nasser who represented a genuinely popular desire for liberalism and modernisation, were seen through Eden's limited patrician perspective as being just like Hitler. Thus Britain was dragged into the humiliating and unsuccessful Suez crisis.

Then there is the Id. We have seen that this creature hates to be thwarted. It is contemptuous of the thought that there can be more than one way of looking at the world. From its point of view, anyone who does not see the world as you see it is a fool or a knave who must be pushed aside or punished accordingly. This, of course, is an unhelpful approach, given the realistic constraints on any manager's power to ignore the wants and perceived needs of others. It is also one that leads losers into much unnecessary expenditure of energy and, often, into the pursuit of dangerous sidetracks where they use their managerial energies to engage in minor vendettas aimed at showing people around them 'who's the boss here'.

The Triad is never more powerful than in its opposition to your need to control and manipulate the people around you as a major function of your managerial life. However, no subject in the study of management will pay you higher dividends.

Personal Experience Exercise

$ Can you think of an occasion when you have seen a manager use coercion to get his way, when the more subtle approach of bribery would have been more effective?

$ Have you ever watched someone be persuaded to do something he would otherwise not do, because of the pay-off it would bring?

SHAPING

If you are going to buy the souls of those about you in your organisation, you need to understand the way in which people's behaviour can be changed. Unlike the direct confrontational approach favoured by Mephistopheles, you can use more subtle methods which have the advantage of being invisible to the victim. They allow you to shape someone's behaviour without his realising that he has been subject to your influence. How do you go about this?

We need to begin by looking at the results of the early experiments carried out by the Russian psychologist Pavlov on the behaviour of dogs.[4] You will no doubt have heard about Pavlov and his dogs, but you probably never thought that they could be allies in your endeavour to be a winner. However, Pavlov's experiments provide the basis for understanding how all animals, including human beings, can have their behaviour moulded.

Pavlov discovered by accident that his charges who, between horrible surgical experiments on their brains, were kept in a darkened kennel, began to show the behaviour associated with eating, salivating—that is dribbling—as soon as the kennel maids put on the kennel light at feeding time. The unfortunate animals had come to transfer the behaviour that is normally attached to the actual presence of food with a symbol that represented food to them by association. The process that Pavlov had stumbled upon was that of 'conditioned reflex', a means of inducing behaviour through the use of a stimulus.

By substituting bells for lights and different pitches of bells for each other, he found that animals applied the normal reflexes of behaviour to a variety of stimuli. These stimuli worked, even when they were eventually divorced from the original stimulus, food itself. Thus, his dogs dribbled when the light went on or his bells sounded, even though the reward originally associated with the behaviour had ceased to be given. After a time, the conditioned behaviour began to drop off: the dogs dribbled less, the longer they were exposed to the lights or bells without the reward of food. In showing how the behaviour of his dogs could be shaped, Pavlov was pioneering the way for managers who wish to buy the souls of those on whom they rely to get their way.

Pavlov's work concentrated on natural reflexes. B. F. Skinner[5] went much farther. He showed that complex patterns of behaviour could be induced by the careful use of reward. In other words, he led the way in showing how behaviour can be shaped using what he called 'reinforcement'—the reward of responses desired by the person wanting to control behaviour. Thus, my terrier still licks her lips when she comes running in answer to the dog whistle, although she has long ceased to get a chocolate drop every time she responds.

Skinner's method is simple. Individuals have needs and they will act to satisfy them. Actions that are successful in meeting these needs will be repeated. This holds true even for quite complex sets of actions linked together to form a behaviour pattern, which have led to reward over a period. On the other hand, negatively rewarded experiences—those resulting in unpleasant consequences—will tend to be avoided. As I write at three o'clock on a Sunday morning, a group of yobs have returned for the third time to call, with increasing disregard for the peace of the neighbourhood, for my neighbour to let them in. Their success will no doubt induce them to use this method of summoning Alec again.

On the other hand, the stone that an exasperated neighbour has just thrown through the window from which Alec agreed to admit them will have a bearing upon the likely outcome of such future summonses.

Although the process of shaping may be conscious during the early stages of what is in effect learning, the result of the

STIMULUS→RESPONSE→REINFORCEMENT→REPEATED BEHAVIOUR

linkage will soon become unconscious and spontaneous. The process of internalisation forms patterns of behaviour that are not easily broken or forgotten, and the rewarded or reinforced behaviour will soon begin to take on a life of its own, relying upon the unconscious memory of reward to feed it. It will become part of the individual's normal behaviour, a habit. This is kept alive by reinforcement, but reward does not have to be issued automatically every time the individual does what is required. Intermittent reinforcement, the reward of desired behaviour every so often, is a powerful and inexpensive means of ensuring that people stay conditioned and, in this respect at least, their souls remain bought.

PSYCHOLOGICAL WAGES

Later in this chapter we shall look at the sorts of things that might be used as rewards in the behaviour conditioning process. At this stage it is necessary to make the important point that non-material rewards—'psychological wages'—are a stronger, cheaper and more readily available method of reinforcing behaviour than are extrinsic and tangible rewards. Only a confirmed loser could seriously ignore such a winning combination. For those who doubt the existence of psychological wages, let me draw an example from the world of driving. Simply think how you feel when you receive a waved thank you from a fellow motorist to whom you have conceded right of way. You feel good, if only for a few moments. You return the wave and you are certainly more likely to repeat the action as a consequence. For a more considered example, take the experiments carried out by J. B. Wolfe.[6]

Wolfe wanted to explore the effects of positive reward upon effort put into work. He chose to carry out a series of experiments involving our near relatives, the chimpanzees. You will not have to work hard to extrapolate from these to see their parallels with human behaviour. Wolfe built a 'work machine', a replica of the old prison treadmill. His chimps were rewarded with grapes after having put in a given amount of work on the wheel and the experimenter found that it did not take much to get his subjects to see that the more they worked on the wheel, the more they were rewarded.

The next stage of the experiment began the process of moving to a form of psychological wages. Wolfe built a grape dispenser that was operated by the insertion of tokens, rather like the machines that sell chocolate at railway stations. The chimpanzees were shown how to operate this device. They then began to be rewarded for their work on the treadmill, not with grapes themselves but with tokens that could be exchanged for grapes from the grape dispenser. The result was interesting. The pace of work increased. The reward of grape tokens was clearly a stronger motivator than the physical reward itself.

Wolfe then took one final step in moving from physical to psychological wages. He varied the 'pay-out' on the grape dispenser. One would expect the chimps to work less as the pay-out became less certain. In fact the opposite was true. The playing of what was literally a fruit machine became obsessive for the chimps. This was true even when Wolfe reduced the pay-out to one grape as little as once in a hundred. So keen were they to earn tokens that they could gamble for grapes, that the animals began to work on the treadmill to the extent that they started to show signs of physical breakdown and the experiments were stopped. Chimpanzees may or may not have souls, but their behaviour was clearly bought by Wolfe who got them to work to the point of near exhaustion by the substitution of psychological wages, non-material rewards, for material ones.

Many managers have difficulty accepting the notion of psychological wages. The idea contradicts conventional management thinking and its belief in money as the only incentive. This fiction has a long pedigree, but it is also a dangerous one. It is important enough to be dealt with in detail later in this chapter, but you should think about its falsehood now. To see the truth, all you have to do is look around you and observe people doing things for rewards that are not explicable in terms of money. Mephistopheles tried the promise of riches to buy the soul of the unfortunate Faust, but it was a desire for knowledge and power that finally ensnared him. The British Civil Service has long understood the principle behind this process. Traditionally it has overcome the problem of attracting high calibre people without having the money to pay them adequately, by ensuring that their jobs carry a high status and that public honours, including titles, are attainable by those who do well in the system. In the process of getting people to do what you want them to do, there are many currencies. Certainly physical reward, in the form of money, is important. However, only a loser would fail to recognise the power of non-material rewards which are cheap and easy to administer and, as we have seen above, potentially more effective.

Personal Experience Exercise

$ Think of a time when you felt good about something. What rewards did you receive that made you feel good?

$ Have you ever been in a job in which you have been well paid yet unhappy?

REWARD VERSUS PUNISHMENT

Another topic vital to the winning manager's understanding of the process of shaping behaviour is the role of punishment. One of the favourite activities of the Super Ego is the meting out of punishment for breaches by others of its own internalised rules. The Super Ego often looks for an excuse, however slim, to vent its pent-up energy and frustrations on those around it. Punishment is a successful way of doing just this. As we have seen from Skinner, successful behaviour, that is behaviour that leads to satisfaction, is very likely to be repeated. If punishment makes us feel better by releasing our pent-up energy, then we shall be likely to go for punishing behaviour on future occasions. We may search for opportunities to use punishment as a means of releasing our inner tensions. And the world of the manager provides many opportunities for us to indulge our predilections. Andrzej Huczynski and David Buchanan,[7] for example, quote Charles O'Reilly and Barton Weitz in finding that some supervisors in their study of junior management 'acquired the taste' for sacking employees. The process of punishing subordinates may become an obsession for managers who do not realise that they are merely finding excuses to indulge the uncontrolled dictates of their Super Egos. Would-be winners need to beware that they do not fall into the trap of using punishment where it is counterproductive to their aims.

A major problem with punishment is that losers see it as the way to get things done. Listen to any group of managers boasting about their successes: sooner or later, talk will get around to how tough they are. While they will tell you that they believe in being 'firm but fair', and that their managerial style is based upon using 'the carrot and the stick', it is their firmness and their skill with the stick about which they will boast. This notion of the need for tough management is so ingrained that when I ask groups of students to choose between two courses of action, giving them one minute in which they can either praise one employee for good performance or admonish another for poor performance, they regularly choose the course of punishment in preference to positive reward.

Punishment clearly has its place in managerial life, but its place is in setting absolute limits of acceptable behaviour –

in stopping people from doing that which they simply must not do. For example, it would be appropriate where the safety of individuals or even the organisation itself might otherwise be put in jeopardy. However, at best, it will gain only people's compliance. The danger is that if used as an everyday response to action that is not a serious threat to your managerial success, it will make people avoid any form of initiative in case they 'get it in the neck' for making minor mistakes. Punishment, meted out unthinkingly, teaches people to 'play safe'. As a winning manager, you cannot afford to be content with this. You are looking to buy people's souls; you want them to do what you want willingly, without realising that they would want to do anything else.

We began this discussion with the shaping of the behaviour of dogs, and it is appropriate to continue by taking examples from dog training, which provides good and easily explained instances of the way behaviour can be shaped. Remember that the principles that apply to the training of animals apply equally well to human behaviour.

The next two diagrams represent two different approaches. Taking a specific case, let us say they represent the process of shaping a dog's behaviour so that it learns to bring its master's slippers when told, 'Fetch slippers'. The key to the diagrams is:

x —positive reinforcement = reward
* —negative reinforcement = punishment
o —no reinforcement = ignoring the action
p —positive reinforcement = non-material reward

Take a punishment-based approach first:

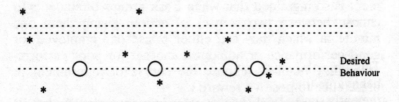

Here the emphasis is upon negative reinforcement for behaviour that is not desired (*). Behaviour that lies on the path towards the behaviour is ignored (o), while behaviour that is not on that path is punished, whether it is outside the limits of tolerable behaviour or just not required as part of the shaping process. A narrative for the diagram might go:

At successive repetitions of the command, 'Fetch slippers':
 Dog urinates on carpet   — * negative reinforcement
 Dog picks up newspaper — * negative reinforcement
 Dog picks up slippers   — o no reinforcement
 Dog picks up pipe   — o no reinforcement
 Dog picks up pipe   — * negative reinforcement

At the beginning of the shaping process the dog is thoroughly confused. It receives punishment for all sorts of things. Being intelligent it avoids what has been punished before. It spends its time learning not what it must do but what it must not do. Then suddenly, from being allowed on one occasion to pick up the pipe, it is now punished for doing so. Perhaps picking up the slippers might be punished next time too. Perhaps picking anything up is likely to be punished! This process of trial and error might just, in time, make the dog realise what is required of it. In addition, however, it will have acquired a whole lot of neuroses.

Contrast this approach with one based upon reward:

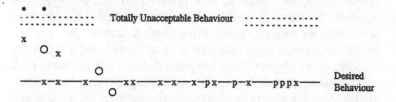

This time the emphasis is upon positive reinforcement for behaviour that is desired (x). Behaviour that lies on or, in the early stages, near the path towards the desired behaviour is rewarded. Behaviour that is not on that path is ignored (o), unless it lies outside the limits of tolerable behaviour when it receives negative reinforcement (*). This time the narrative might be:

At successive repetitions of the command, 'Fetch slippers':

Dog urinates on carpet	— * negative reinforcement
Dog sniffs at slippers	— x positive reinforcement
Dog chews computer disk	— * negative reinforcement
Dog picks up pipe	— o no reinforcement
Dog sniffs slippers	— x positive reinforcement
Dog picks up pipe	— o no reinforcement
Dog picks up slippers	— x positive reinforcement
Dog sniffs slippers	— o no reinforcement
Dog picks up slippers	— x positive reinforcement
Dog fetches slippers	— x positive reinforcement.
Dog fetches slippers	— p Non-material reward.

This time, right from the start of the behaviour shaping process, the limits of acceptable behaviour are set. However, a distinction is clearly made between behaviour that must be totally eradicated and behaviour that is irrelevant. At the beginning, any behaviour related to the slippers is rewarded. Later on it is only the action of picking up the slippers that receives positive attention. Later still, only the act of fetching the slippers will be rewarded. Very soon the dog will have absorbed the behaviour into its normal repertoire and master will get his slippers every time. Note that once the pattern of desired behaviour—fetching the slippers—has begun to be established, it is possible to use non-material rewards to keep it going. Dogs, for example, in common with human beings, need attention. A gentle pat on the head, the canine equivalent of a 'thank you', will eventually become reward enough to keep the desired behaviour active.

The same principles apply in shaping human behaviour. In the second diagram above, punishment is only administered at the limits of acceptable behaviour, when it is likely to bring severe consequences. There may be narrow or broad limits, according to the nature of the work involved, but punishment is not invoked until those limits are crossed. Then it must be invoked quickly, to make the link between the behaviour and the punishment clear. You will likewise use reward to mark the path to required behaviour. In the diagram above, every time behaviour falls on or near the path towards the desired behaviour, it is rewarded in such a way that there is a clear link between desired behaviour and positive reward. From the evidence, the desired behaviour will become normal and natural after a short time. All you have to do is remember to reward it every so often, using positive reinforcement.

It is worth repeating that positive reward does not need to be tangible. Mere acknowledgement that they are on the right path to the desired behaviour is usually enough for human subjects.

Personal Experience Exercise
$ Can you think of an occasion where the threat of punishment has made you play safe?

SPECIFICITY

A serious problem with the learning process is that the wrong things are often learnt by accident. Just as Pavlov's dogs came to associate light with food, people often link part of the environment that is present at the time reward or punishment takes place and have their behaviour shaped in a direction that is not wanted. Hans Eysenck gives an excellent example of this process in his book *Fact and Fiction in Psychology*.[8]

Eysenck shows how male sexual impotency is usually a learnt phenomenon. Men can bring unconscious negative associations to the sex act and their bodies react to help them avoid the physical state necessary to perform it. In one example he tells of a French lorry driver who was being treated for impotency. The problem, however, was only related to sexual relations with his wife. Under hypnosis, the man revealed that he had once been caught making love to the wife of a fellow lorry driver. For this he received a severe thrashing. His marital problem stemmed from the fact that the thrashing took place in a bedroom with a distinctive pattern of wallpaper. His own marital bedroom, coincidentally, had wallpaper of the same unusual pattern. The negative reinforcement that resulted from the beating attached itself not as 'Thou shalt not covet thy neighbour's wife', but as 'Thou shalt not make love to anyone's wife, including thine own, in a room with this wallpaper'. A quick DIY job sorted out the man's marriage. As an interesting aside, Eysenck felt it necessary to explain that the wallpaper was a problem because the story took place in France where sexual relations are conducted with the light on.

Eysenck's story indicates that you should not leave reward, or indeed punishment, to chance but should make sure that these are specifically attached to given behaviours. A useful tool is the use of praise, saying 'Thank you' and 'Well done' to highlight behaviour that you want to be repeated. Praise homes in on the specific parts of behaviour to be rewarded and thus shaped. It is a potentially powerful reinforcer; however, it is cheap and easy to use in close association with the desired behaviour.

Losers have a problem with this idea. 'Real men don't eat quiche', as the title of a popular satire on male touchiness about 'correct' macho behaviour would have us believe. That book might have included in its list of things to be avoided the use of the phrases 'please' and 'thank you', at least as far as the behaviour of a lot of managers goes. Again, we have here an example of the Triad forces trying to lure potential winners of the organisation game astray. For the Id, keen to assert its power over its entire environment, the use of such politeness will seem an admission of weakness, of self-doubt, of softness in the face of those only too ready to take advantage of any momentary lapse of a strong guard. For the Ego it will seem unnecessary: people do what they have to do in organisations because they are rational and see that they have to get on with their job. For the Super Ego, as we have seen, punishment is often the preferred motivator. The Super Ego expects people to know what is right or wrong and they should not need praise or thanks for behaving 'properly'.

Only a loser would prefer to be deflected from winning by the dictates of the Triad. You, as a winner, can stand apart from these urges and keep both eyes firmly on the goal of getting your own way by whatever means are available.

Personal Experience Exercise

$ Can you think of a time when a 'thank you' would have made all efforts seem worthwhile?

$ Think of an occasion when you praised a subordinate. Did you notice any difference in his or her behaviour afterwards?

$ Do you know someone who always picks on what is wrong but never supports the good things that you and your people do?

MOTIVATION

So far we have talked about the need to buy the souls of those around you in order to gain power over your life in the organisation. It is now time to consider the currencies that you can use in order to achieve your aim. To this end you need an understanding of human motivation.

A useful way of approaching this study is to look at the origin of the word 'motivation' itself. It comes from the Latin verb *movere*, and from an etymological standpoint is the study of what makes people 'move'. It follows that once you understand this you can investigate the problem of 'how to get people to move'—in the direction you require. One of the leading writers on the subject, Frederick Herzberg, sees the manager's job as getting his subordinates to 'jump for jelly beans'. Clearly, he would be at one with Mephistopheles in his view that people's souls can be bought. It is a matter of finding out what will buy them—what flavour of jelly beans will make each of them jump.[9]

The study of motivation starts from the premise that those

trying to influence others have a set of desired outcomes. For you, these relate to attaining your vision, but the people you must try to influence also have needs which you can help them to fulfil through control of the rewards that the organisation can offer. The secret of getting people to do what you want comes from your ability to link their self-interest with the attainment of the outcomes that you want for yourself. Your problem lies in identifying the interests and goals of others, for the reality often differs from the perception.

Most managers hold their jobs because of their ability to get things done quickly and effectively. The system that has promoted them to positions of responsibility has done so on the basis of results. Neither they nor the organisations that promoted them have considered the mechanisms used to achieve these, but the practicalities will have led them to develop a pragmatic approach to their dealing with people. Whatever gets results, whatever leads to success in getting the job done, will be repeated. Strategies that seem likely to fail will be avoided.

Douglas McGregor, in his seminal work *The Human Side of Enterprise*,[10] sums up very well this development of a 'managerial unconsciousness', showing how managers come to see the people that they are to manage in a particular light; from this they take a generalised view of human behaviour which, in turn, will determine their approach to the problem of gaining the compliance of subordinates.

How do you see the people you manage?

Try this test. Do not spend more than two minutes over it. Give your quick and instinctive response to the statements listed, marking each with a score from 0 to 4:

　　4—if you strongly agree
　　3—if you tend to agree
　　2—if you are undecided
　　1—if you tend to disagree
　　0—if you strongly disagree

STATEMENTS	SCORE
My staff like the fact that I am always ready to show the best way of getting the job done	—
If I, or someone like me, were not in control, little would get done	—
My staff expect me to set their goals and objectives for them	—
I check every day that my staff are coping with their work	—
I keep a close check to see that my staff are punctual in their attendance	—
My staff work best when they are rewarded for their efforts by high pay.	—
I am always pushing my people to meet deadlines	—
I hold frequent meetings so I am always in touch	—
My staff want me to take the important decisions myself	—
My staff would avoid the difficult tasks, if someone was not constantly on the look-out	—
I am always there to step in as soon as things seem to get behind	—
I like to know what my staff are doing, all the time	—
My staff want me to take the responsibility for planning their work for them	—
I set up close checks to see that my staff are keeping up with the job	—
I keep a close watch on my staff so as to ensure I get the best out of them	—
TOTAL SCORE=	——

Remember your total score and we shall come back to it soon!

McGregor describes two ideal types of approach to managing people. The first, which he calls Theory X, is common in managerial thinking. It has its origins in the learning of those who typically have had to control disaffected workforces, working in alienating conditions, where the need has been for short-term results. Against such a background of experience most managers regard their subordinates as sullenly unwilling participants in the production process. According to Theory X, subordinates dislike work intensely and will seek excuses to avoid it; managers therefore need to control them closely and to bribe and coerce them if they want to get things done. At its extreme, this approach justifies itself by the notion that it really does not matter to most employees anyway. People are inherently lazy and apathetic and consequently prefer to be tightly monitored and directed in the workplace.

The problem with this belief is that it becomes what is known as a 'self-fulfilling prophecy'. Clearly, many managers have encountered subordinates who were lazy and lacking in initiative, but these attitudes are themselves a response to the approach of managers. By expecting people to be sullen and passive, managers who unconsciously subscribe to a Theory X view treat them in a way that produces the very orientations they expected in the first place. With their expectations confirmed and rewarded, they are encouraged to continue to exercise Theory X principles, and the whole process becomes locked in a never-ending circle of 'I told you so'.

As a winning manager this approach is not for you. You must wean yourself of the need to get things done quickly through pressure for short-term results, and concentrate instead on long-term success, using McGregor's second ideal type of managerial approach which he called Theory Y. This sees subordinates as potential allies in the business of winning the organisation game.

The Theory Y manager recognises the real facts of human experience. In contrast to the flawed philosophy of the Theory X manager, he realises that people do not naturally dislike work—in fact, if you look at how they really behave, expenditure of effort is part of their normal and natural behaviour. Huw Beynon, in his study of the British Ford motor car plant at Dagenham,[11] a factory managed along strictly Theory X lines, describes how, alienated by the drudgery of the production line, motor car workers spend their breaks playing football in the factory yard. It is clearly not the expenditure of effort that people seek to avoid, but effort under circumstances over which they feel themselves to have no control.

The message from McGregor's work is clear. When committed, when they feel themselves to be 'acting agents in their own grasp of their world', people are perfectly capable of applying their talents to the goal of shifting product. All you need to do to secure their commitment is to learn how to buy their souls.

How do you really see the people you manage?

You have already committed yourself The test that you did just now says it all. The possible total scores range from 0 to 60, representing a continuum from 0 (a Theory Y orientation) to 60 (an extreme Theory X view). Does this correspond with how you would really want to manage?

This is not meant to be a textbook on motivation. There is an abundant literature on the subject of the currencies that managers can use to buy the souls of those on whom they must rely to get things done. My task is to show you, the winning manager, some of the options open to you and to warn you of the traps into which the loser is likely to fall by not understanding the available options. I would recommend, however, that you look at the subject of motivation in more detail, and particularly the relevant chapters of Andrzej Huczynski's and David Buchanan's excellent book *Organisational Behaviour*[12] for a sound treatment of the topic. Here, I intend to concentrate on the principles of motivation only as far as they are directly relevant to your need to buy people's souls to attain your ends.

MASLOW'S HIERARCHY OF NEEDS

The work of Abraham Maslow[13] is vital to understanding the nature of people's self-interest to which we referred on page 136. Discovering individuals' self-interest is the first stage in the process of determining what will induce them to act.

As a result of his researches, Maslow deduced that people's behaviour can be explained by their inner drives to satisfy basic sets of needs. If they are thirsty they seek liquid, if they are hungry they seek food. The more hungry or thirsty they are the more they engage in behaviour that will satisfy these needs.

Hunger and thirst are obvious examples because we can all recognise them easily in people's daily behaviour. Some of the sets of needs that Maslow identified are not so obvious, but despite being less tangible and operating at a level not normally perceptible to the individual, they are equally strong drives. Here is a list of the clusters of needs that Maslow identified. The examples against each of them are not exhaustive but are included to give some flesh to Maslow's findings:

PHYSIOLOGICAL NEEDS
Food, warmth, sex.

SAFETY NEEDS
Shelter, security, order.

SOCIAL NEEDS
Companionship, affection, belonging.

ESTEEM NEEDS
Attention, recognition, reputation.

SELF-REALISATION NEEDS
Self-development, individuality.

From the examples of these needs, they may seem to you to be passive. However, Maslow argues that they operate at a very powerful level. They direct action; they drive people to behave in a way that is likely to fulfil them. Although they operate largely at an unconscious level and people are made conscious of them only when they remain unfulfilled, they also have the power to direct thoughts. Their strength can best be shown by looking at two examples of the effects on behaviour of deprivation. Both come from military life where extreme conditions are likely to be encountered; both concern a physiological need, the need for food, chosen because it provides an easily identifiable illustration. However, the needs under Maslow's other headings are no less strong and they direct people's thoughts and behaviour in the same powerful way.

The first example concerns my own experience of being temporarily out of touch with the military rations system. During a military exercise, my companion and I were required to inhabit a hole in the ground, without stirring from it for a period of three days. We had both missed meals on day one. By an unlucky accident our rations did not catch up with us for two more days. We were both very hungry!

On the third day my companion suddenly looked at me in horror. Apparently, I was dribbling green slime from my mouth. I looked, as he put it, like 'f . . . ing Frankenstein'. When I wiped my chin, sure enough, there was green liquid all over my hands. Then the cause became apparent. Unknown to me, Maslow's drives to action to fulfil my need for food had taken over, and as I stood there in our trench my body had engaged itself in behaviour that was likely to satisfy the overwhelming need of the moment: I had obviously been putting things in my mouth in the hope of finding sustenance. Currently, I was engaged in sucking out the contents of the refill of my green ball-point pen. The power required to do this is extremely great; nevertheless, driven by the need to eat, my body had set up the necessary strong sucking motions. It tasted horrible!

The second example comes from an anecdote told by a survivor of the battle for Stalingrad. He was a sergeant in a small German unit cut off by the Russians and they had eaten no proper food for a week. Their officer ordered a morale-boosting exercise. They were each to give a short talk on the theme 'What I shall do when I go home to Germany after the war'.

When it came to Willi's turn to describe his future away from the threatened horrors of defeat and capture, he began to describe how he intended to buy a little Volkswagen. Every Saturday he would clean it and polish it (it was traditionally illegal to clean your car in public on Sunday in Germany). Then he would open the engine compartment and ... there would be beef olives and gravy ... Everyone, including Willi, laughed riotously at the *non sequitur*. No one realised that what was happening was that Willi's thoughts had been taken over by the powerful compulsion to fulfil his need for food. His inner drives were making sure that the desperate need was kept central to his thoughts, whether Willi wanted this or not.

Maslow's contribution to the understanding of what makes people act did not stop at identifying the drives that govern their behaviour. More importantly for you as a winning manager, he hit upon the key to understanding why people behave differently and how successive generations of managers have tried to buy the compliance of those who work for them, using the wrong currencies.

Maslow argued that the clusters of needs that he identified do not all operate at once. Rather, an individual will have a centre of 'gravity' that will form the basis of his motivation at a given time. This centre of gravity will shift, according to circumstances, but also according to a pattern.

He saw the clusters of needs governing behaviour as arranged in what he called *the hierarchy of needs*, running from physiological needs at the bottom, to self-realisation needs at its peak.

Self-fulfilment
Esteem
Social
Safety
Physiological

At the start individuals have their motivational centre of gravity firmly governed by physiological needs. The factors underlying their behaviour are determined by the need to fulfil their material requirements, or to provide the wherewithal to do so. However, the drives that direct their behaviour will not remain dominated by physiological needs for long. Once these have been partially satisfied, they cease to be the centre of gravity and individuals move onwards and upwards in Maslow's hierarchy, their behaviour driven by the needs drawn from the next cluster. This process will continue to the top of the hierarchy of needs. As long as partial satisfaction of the lower order needs continues to take place, the drives governing behaviour will be those at the top of the hierarchy rather than those at the bottom.

There is a graphic illustration of this process in Daniel Defoe's famous story, *Robinson Crusoe*. The castaway arrives on a remote island. His first actions, driven by physiological needs, are to find food and shelter, and the narrative that Defoe creates for Crusoe shows that he has no place for other thoughts. But once these needs are partially satisfied, he is immediately struck by the fact that he might not be alone for long. Suddenly the centre of gravity of his behaviour becomes the drive to make himself secure from the marauders who might threaten his safety. Only when he has built a fortification which he can defend against all comers does he begin to wish that someone actually might come. Having fulfilled his safety needs, he is now driven by the need for companionship – social needs – and he actively sets about courting danger to rescue Man Friday in order to fulfil this need. The remainder of the island adventure shows him following Maslow's predicted pattern of behaviour. Friday's company is not enough. Motivated by esteem needs, Crusoe proceeds to make Friday subservient to him in his role of feudal lord of his island. But even this is not enough. Having satisfied the other needs on the hierarchy, Crusoe embarks on a self-realisation project to educate Friday.

For managers, the picture drawn by Maslow is inconvenient. It is very comforting to see the people you must motivate as driven only by the lower order needs of the hierarchy, which are easily satisfied by the blanket use of money to fulfil them. This is why losers in the organisation game insist upon maintaining the fiction that people can only be motivated by material rewards. It means that they do not need to consider the difficult business of managing people as individuals who might have needs that are less easily satisfied. However, failure to recognise the reality of what motivates people, what drives them to act, is a dangerous strategy for those who want to buy people's souls rather than their short-term compliance.

People will not be driven by higher order needs while the lower order needs dominate. Once the latter are met they will cease to be useful as a means of getting people to do what you want them to do. Reliance upon the use of lower order needs as a source of motivation is the potential cause, at best, of failure to get results from those on whom you rely to shift product for you. At worst, it leads to alienation or disaffection. The need to take this aspect of Maslow's hierarchy seriously is illustrated by two examples of organisational behaviour that can best be explained by reference to Maslow.

Huw Beynon's book about the organisation of production at the Ford motor plant at Dagenham, cited above,[14] shows workers earning high wages. The Seventies were a time of full employment when skilled workers could expect to find jobs without difficulty. The solidarity of the workplace provided for their social needs and the material rewards of working for Ford gave them a high degree of prestige amongst their peers. Conventional wisdom would lead one to expect that the Ford workforce would be a contented one, happily engaged in shifting the company's product for high material rewards. Beynon's study, however, is full of examples of discontent, unwillingness to work, industrial unrest and even behaviour bordering on sabotage. For example, he describes young men making 'bombs' of glue and throwing them, alight, into waste skips, to produce flames twenty feet high.

The managers in Beynon's study, and even the workers'

representatives themselves, were at a loss to understand why Ford's employees were not content with their lot. The fact was that these workers hated their monotonous jobs, tied to the awfulness of a motor car production line. Their jobs fulfilled all of Maslow's lower order needs and, in doing so, had propelled them towards the need for self-realisation which, by its nature, the work could not satisfy.

The second illustration comes from the Eighties which, in Britain, were a time of massive expansion of the financial services sector. Inevitably, corruption and sharp practice flourished alongside honest trading. The period saw some of the most notorious scandals that the City of London had experienced. One of them involved a market trader, whom I shall call Rupert, because that is not his name.

It was common knowledge in the City that Rupert hated his boring job, despite being paid a six-figure salary. There was always going to be a market for his financial skills. The work was people-based and the team with which he worked formed a close-knit social group. Being one of the leading men in his field, he was highly regarded in the City. In short, all the lower order needs of Maslow's hierarchy were satisfied, but he still hated his job. When he tried to leave, his boss doubled his already enormous salary. Rupert stayed on, despite the fact that, like Beynon's car workers, he had no scope to meet the need that now drove him—self-realisation. Six months later, the Department of Trade and Industry conducted a major investigation into one of the deals in which Rupert had been a major protagonist. He and his colleagues, unable to get the satisfaction they sought from their work, had set out to 'beat the system', not for financial reward but for its own sake. His company was fined and Rupert will never be allowed to trade on a British stock market again.

Both examples forcibly make the same point. In both, the subjects had been involved in work that had pushed the centre of gravity of their motivation to the top of Maslow's hierarchy. Those who managed them, however, thought only in terms of extrinsic, material rewards as a way of involving their subordinates in the product-shifting process. In neither case did it occur to the managers that, while they had bought compliance, they had not bought their employees' souls. Instead, they relied upon the traditional management recipe for trying to involve those who work for them—paying more money. Money was not the source of the problem; indeed it aggravated it, locking both the Ford workers and Rupert into 'golden handcuffs'. Alienated from their jobs, they had no scope to fulfil their needs for self-fulfilment. Yet they could not afford to give up the high material rewards that derived from those jobs. Without a means of satisfaction that would buy their souls for their employers, they found their own, destructive ways of obtaining that satisfaction.

Personal Experience Exercise
$ Can you think of a time when you could not concentrate on something because you were hungry or thirsty?
$ Do you know someone who has a well-paid job but hates his work?
$ Have you ever been tempted to swap your job for a more fulfilling one that paid less?

BUYING SOULS

By now I hope that you are convinced of your need for people's collaboration in your pursuit of power in the organisation, and realise that these theories of using what you know about their needs on one hand, and ways that can be used to gain power over them by shaping their behaviour on the other, must form part of your thinking at every stage of the business of managing. In dealing with individuals it is no use behaving as though everyone about you will be motivated by the same rewards. As we have seen, different people will have different needs to be fulfilled and you must be flexible enough to find out what will buy each individual's effective collaboration.

You cannot, however, approach the business of buying

souls as a set of one-off transactions between manager and managed. You must design the working environment so that your subordinates' motivational needs are satisfied while they are working on your behalf.

Frederick Herzberg[15] offers a practical solution to the problem of designing and maintaining this type of environment. His ideas provide an outline blueprint for buying the souls of people in the organisation and making sure that they stay bought. He argues that you must approach the problem in two ways.

First, you must ensure that the workplace offers scope for the satisfaction of the lower order needs that Maslow identified. Herzberg sees money, status and security as being vital areas of concern in this process. If you want people to shift product for you:

- Pay them adequately.
- Allow them to feel that they have a recognised and worthwhile status in the organisation.
- Make them feel that their position is capable of being as secure as the uncertainties of the economic environment can permit.

The physical conditions need to be the best that the type of work will allow. Some jobs are inherently dirty, dangerous or stressful. Nevertheless, you must not let this become an excuse for working conditions to be more uncomfortable than is absolutely necessary.

You must then address the social environment of the workplace. If your subordinates are to satisfy their social needs, the interpersonal relationships must be conducive to a good working atmosphere. A major part of this managerial task is to ensure that managers themselves do not foul the working environment by officious and autocratic behaviour that has more to do with releasing their own Super Ego drive to exert control, or even to punish people about them, than with achieving results.

None of this, however, will buy the souls of your subordinates. Vital as these concerns are, they will not produce a fully motivated workforce. In Maslow's terms, getting these things right will only deal with the lower order needs of his hierarchy and leave the higher order needs of self-realisation unattended. *Satisfy the higher order needs and you will be able to buy the souls of those who work for you.* Get them wrong and, as Maslow shows, you won't get the required results.

Herzberg's recipe is therefore to use the powerful psychological wages that come from the top of Maslow's hierarchy, self-realisation. The working environment that you control must offer opportunities for everyone in it to fulfil their own higher order needs. People need to gain a sense of achievement from their work; they need to see that what you set them to do has a purpose that they can fulfil and take a pride in. When designing work you must consider these factors, even when dealing with menial jobs.

People need an opportunity for personal growth. They need to be able to feel that they are, in however small a way, responsible for their immediate working environment, rather than being carried along in some impersonal process over which they have no control. Most importantly, they need to be able to draw on that most powerful of all sources of psychological wages—recognition. If you want people to achieve results for you, you must give them the opportunity to feel not only that they contribute to the greater scheme of the work of the organisation, but that their contribution is recognised and that they themselves are valued. Do this and people will shift the product for you that will make you a winner.

Personal Experience Exercise

$ Have you ever asked yourself, 'What have I done this week?'

$ Do you work better when you feel you are in control of your environment?

$ Have you ever felt a glow of satisfaction when your boss has recognised the effort you have put in?

$ Have you ever felt an inner voice saying, with pride, 'I did part of that'?

The following example illustrates the point of this chapter. Old Seth had set up his factory after World War II. During the war he had learnt how to make electricity work to save labour. With the money he had saved, he bought a lease on the top floor of a redundant spinning mill and started a factory that produced electric kettles. They sold like hot cakes and Seth soon made a lot of money.

By the early Seventies he had had enough of work. His sons had shunned the business to go into the professions, but his grandson came from a generation that considered manufacturing a worthwhile career. Old Seth therefore retired to his hobbies and handed over to young Seth.

What young Seth discovered, when he looked at the company books, horrified him. The firm was barely making a profit. It had only continued to operate through large injections from previous profits. In recent years old Seth had run the firm not as a profit-making enterprise, but as an expensive hobby.

There seemed to be no rational production system. The work was organised in ways that had been developed to meet a particular need, now long passed. Above all, there was no proper control over production rates and quality. Young Seth set about changing all this.

The workforce was largely made up of women earning a second income. To young Seth, they seemed to treat the factory more like a social club than a productive enterprise: there was a lot of gossiping but not enough work being done. The answer was to install a proper production line. Each woman would carry out one small task on a kettle and pass it on for the next process by means of a newly purchased conveyor belt. To ensure concentration on kettle-making rather than chatter, each worker was given her own booth, cut off from her neighbours by a six-foot partition.

Young Seth introduced one final refinement. Under the old system, the women would go to the stores to collect the parts and materials they needed. Here they would have a leisurely chat to Joe, the one-legged storeman, and smoke a cigarette before going back to their work benches.

Under the new system, Joe would do the rounds with a trolley, dropping off the parts to the workers.

To Seth's delight, production rates soared. But there were problems in store. For the first time ever, the firm's products began to be returned as faulty. When a proper system of quality control was set up, an unacceptable percentage of kettles had to be scrapped as not up to standard. The 'people' side of the firm also began to deteriorate. Women who had worked for old Seth for years began to leave. Newcomers needed recruitment and training, all of which took up valuable management time. The sickness and absence rates soared. This had never been a problem under the old regime. Now, a large amount of production time was being lost. The women, whose families relied upon the second income for luxuries, had become disenchanted with a working environment that gave them nothing beyond material reward.

Determined not to lose face in front of his grandfather, Seth invited a firm of management consultants to help him out of his difficulties. With their knowledge of how people's souls are bought, they came up with the following solutions, based on the ideas we have looked at in this book:

- Scrap the booths and encourage groups of friends to sit together and talk while they work. If you can let work fulfil people's social needs, this will make them want to be part of the production process and capitalise on the notion of facilitation.
- Scrap the production line. Instead of each worker doing one small task in isolation, let everyone make a whole kettle. People want to see that their efforts lead to something meaningful. Three hundred handles screwed on is not meaningful; thirty kettles made by one's own hand is.
- Let the women collect their own parts. The chance to take a break from their work has two effects. Firstly, people work better when a monotonous routine can be broken up. More importantly, they work better when they feel they have control over their own pace of work.
- Introduce flexible working hours. The particular type of

worker in Seth's firm has other pressing calls on her
time—children and family. Allowing these to fit into the
production routine offers her a yet greater feeling that
she can be personally responsible for her own working
life. Therefore introduce job sharing and flexitime.

- Identify the kettles that each woman makes. For quality
control reasons it is useful to trace faults back to their
source. Give each worker her own labels that are to be
soldered to her kettles. However, over and above this,
such personalisation increases the stake that each woman
feels in the firm's output. When the main market for a
firm's product is in the street markets of the locality, as
in Seth's case, the workers and their families are known
and people will check the labels on kettles to see if they
know who made them.

And the company went from strength to strength.

7 Leaders Win

A proactive approach is essential if you are to be a winning manager. In the words of the American managerial slogan, it requires an attitude of GOYA—'Get off your hindquarters'.

Implicit in this approach is the imperative for you to find ways to release the will to win that is locked up in your Id and combine this with a new set of Super Ego rules that stress winning on your terms. The will to be a winning manager is not enough on its own. In short, the domination of the managerial environment and the people who inhabit it cannot be achieved by the mere exercise of will: it requires will to be translated into *leadership*.

The study of leadership is about finding how winning managers are most likely to achieve positive results in the organisation. It concerns how to make decisions and implement them effectively. Leadership is the difficult business of shifting product, given that you have to rely upon others to work for you. And, as we have seen, the cooperation and compliance of others is far from guaranteed. In this book the subject is examined in terms of how it can help you impose your will on your environment.

As with all areas of management on which we have touched, the study of leadership is full of dangerous notions that will, if left unchecked, lead you in the wrong direction. More than any other aspect of management area, it has been associated with a whole range of 'crap ideas', most of which have originated in the manager's psyche.

Mention the word 'leadership' and managers are reduced to a state of religious awe. Leadership is sacred, a holy grail for the aspiring manager. Leaders are an 'elite' with 'extraordinary' qualities. And any hint that an individual manager may not have the qualities of leadership is taken as an affront to his very conception of himself. Managers seem to regard the possession of leadership rather as most men regard their manhood—any question of its possession evokes an immediate defensive response.

Personal Experience Exercise
$ What do you understand by the term 'leadership'?
$ Make a list of the characteristics that you think make a good leader.

Most people think of leadership as a set of personal characteristics. Here are some of the qualities that surround the concept, taken both from some of the writing on the subject,[1] and from asking managers to define leadership:

charisma	humour
concern for people	integrity
courage	intelligence
fairness	judgement
firmness	knowledge
flexibility	trustworthiness
honour	will power

Think about them. They read like a list of ideal character traits for prospective applicants to the Boy Scouts. They tell you nothing about how to lead people. Try to apply the list to some successful leaders from the world of international affairs and you will see what I mean. Think about Ronald Reagan's charisma, Joseph Stalin's concern for people, Edouard Balladour's courage, Adolf Hitler's fairness, Margaret Thatcher's flexibility, and so on and so on. Most of these successful leaders lack some if not most of the traits from this or any other list. Moreover, it is by no means certain that any individual who has all the traits in the list will actually be any good at the business of getting people to do things for him. The problem with the 'qualities' approach is that it produces definitions of leadership that are impossible to apply as models in the real world.

The above list of personal characteristics should be dismissed by any manager who wants to be a winner. Concentration on the notion of leadership emphasises the macho 'I am the boss' approach which, as we shall see, is only one of the possible strategies that you can use to get people to shift product. There are, in fact a number of different approaches to the making and implementation of decisions in organisations; and you need to understand which style is appropriate for each set of circumstances.

A more practical approach is the one adopted by John Adair in his work *Training for Leadership*.[2] Adair defines the manager's role as being responsible for ensuring that his team's task is carried out. He argues that the leader can best achieve this by dividing the task into three areas, as illustrated in the figure opposite. He also needs to weld his team into a cohesive unit, using the characteristics of people who want to belong to a group for his benefit. But this is not, in itself, enough to galvanise people into action. Concern for individual needs is Adair's third ingredient. This is where a knowledge of how to buy individual team members' souls comes into its own. The winning manager knows his people and learns how to buy their support and enthusiasm for his ends. Adair sees successful leaders as being those who can balance these three tasks in order to shift product effectively. His approach is shown diagrammatically in the figure:[3]

As a winning manager you need to recognise that different situations require different styles of behaviour. Losers, obsessed by the 'qualities' approach and their need to avoid showing signs of weakness, will stick to a style of behaviour that seems to show them to everybody, including themselves, as the Big Boss. You, however, will use a number of styles that achieve your ends more subtly. You will be more concerned with achieving results than with improving your managerial hardness in pursuit of a Super Ego image of how macho managers ought to behave.

Once you focus on an approach such as Adair's, you can reject the illusory quest for the Boy Scout qualities of the

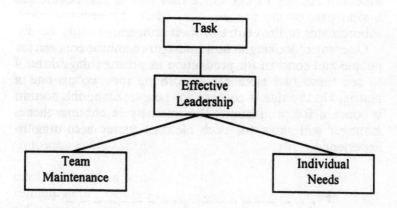

'good leader' and concentrate instead on the process of discovering what sort of behaviour is required of you to perform effectively.

THE TASK AND PEOPLE

Most managers have little or no training in the art of managing and come to their offices because they have been successful in the business of shifting product. They rely therefore upon the age-old method of learning their jobs by doing what seems to have been successful, either in past jobs or for their predecessors in their current job. They very rarely consider whether there might be a more effective way of achieving their aims.

Some managers, who do not think seriously about the art of managing people, consider the task to be more important than the other concerns that Adair highlights: individual needs and team maintenance. Those new to the business may even assume that any other style of managerial behaviour will undermine their credibility amongst their subordinates and their peers—'real managers are task-orientated managers'! Other managers, who may have been taken in by some of the less useful theories that abound in the field of managerial literature, may have focused on the people

aspect of Adair's model. Once they realise that people are
a vital part of the process, they place the needs of their
subordinates at the centre of their concern.

One way of looking at how managers combine concern for
people and concern for production in getting things done is
to see these two elements as forming the two axes of a
matrix. Up the side is concern for people; along the bottom
is concern for production. The intensity of concern that a
manager will show for each element varies according to
experience:

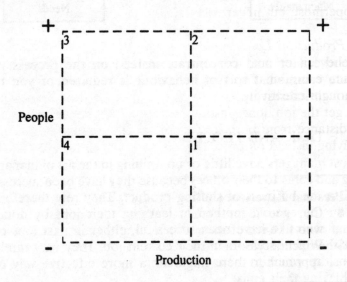

Using this matrix it is possible to identify four typical managerial styles:

1 *Production High/People Low*
This type sees the needs of people and the needs of production systems as incompatible. Production is more important than the needs of people.

2 *Production High/People High*

For this manager there is no conflict between production and people needs. By the exercise of skilful management, the needs of people can be linked to production without jeopardy to either.

3 *Production Low/People High*

This type resembles what Robert Blake and Jane Mouton referred to as the 'country club' manager.[4] For him, the emphasis is upon people and their needs. Without this, production is not possible and the needs of his team will be uppermost, but never exclusive, in his management style.

4 *Production Low/People Low*

Believe it or not, this style of management orientation is quite common. This type of manager will, of course, take enough interest in both elements to satisfy the basic need to get the job done. Instinctively, however, he will maintain a distance from both his team and the production system, relying instead on procedures.

Personal Experience Exercise
$ Can you identify managers in your organisation who fit each of these four typical styles?
$ Which style do you think best describes your approach to managing people?

From looking at this matrix you may think that there is one preferable style which all winning managers should adopt for all occasions. Certainly, you may be forgiven for questioning the place in the organisation for the fourth style— production low/people low. However, Paul Hershey and Kenneth Blanchard[5] would dispute such a blanket prescription of appropriate management styles. They have developed a theory which takes into account the maturity of the work group to be managed and argue that there is a different style for each stage of maturity. Here I have developed upon this theory in the following way. Where possible, the work of a manager should be divided into projects, each having a distinct beginning, an intermediate phase and a continuation phase. In this development from Hershey and Blanchard it is the maturity of a project, rather than of the work group, that attracts different styles of management. The following diagram plots the balance of concern for people and production from right to left, through the developing maturity of a project.

Project Life Cycle

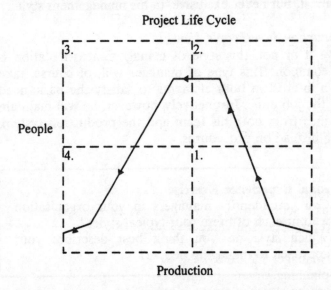

People

Production

At the beginning of a project the main priority is to set up the technology of the production system. The style of management at this stage of the project life cycle is one that emphasises task and production. Human relationships are not yet a major issue. Unlike Hershey and Blanchard's model of group maturity, however, I would argue that concern for people's needs should never be excluded from the mind of the manager and you will note that, even at the start of the

project life cycle, the need for orientation towards people's
needs is never totally absent. However, very soon the the
cycle, people are required to become involved. This requires
a style of management that emphasises the relationship
between achieving the needs of production on one hand and
satisfying the needs of individuals and the group on the other.

As the project develops, the emphasis shifts strongly
towards a style of management that is people orientated.
The technology of the production system has been
developed and people have been trained in getting it right.
What is now required is a management style that can maintain the momentum by developing and maintaining the
team. Lastly, as the project reaches maturity, the efforts of
the manager can be relaxed. Production has been allied
to the team's needs and the project can proceed with
minimum intervention by the manager who can devote his
efforts to the earlier phases of the other projects in his
portfolio.

There are two ways that this notion of project life cycle
and management style can be exploited in your organisation.
First, by reference to it, you can recognise what is required
of you in terms of effort. You must learn to recognise your
strengths and your weaknesses together with your preferences for particular aspects of managerial activity. You must
then take action to ensure that, despite your weaknesses
and preferences, your management style is appropriate to
the phase that a given project has reached. The four tasks
of the manager identified by Herbert Hicks and Ray Gullett[6]—planning, organising, motivating and controlling—can
therefore be assigned to the stages of the project life cycle
as shown on p. 160.

A second and more imaginative way of exploiting the
knowledge gained from the concept of the project life cycle
is to 'play to your strengths'. Rather than attempting to be
a good all-round manager, capable of applying all the styles
of management appropriate to each phase of a project's
maturity, you can become a specialist at what you do well.
Thus, if you have a low people orientation and a high concern for production, you might make a career in planning;

Project Life Cycle

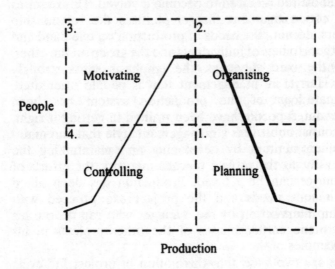

Production

if you see yourself as a 'country club' man, you could find your talents best used in the motivating phases of projects.

DECIDING AND IMPLEMENTING

Another option is to plan your decisions in the form of a continuum of responsibilities:

Manager - - - - - - - - Team

At one end of this continuum, you make the decisions. You then announce what is to be done and how it is to be accomplished. At the other end, the entire business is left to your team of subordinates to make the decisions. Between these two extremes, there exists an infinite number of possibilities concerning the level of your involvement and that of your subordinates. Despite the beliefs of many losers, there is an appropriate time and place for the different styles of behaviour across this continuum.

Before we go any farther, we need to know what is meant

by 'subordinates' in our discussion of leadership styles. Those managers who have internalised Theory X assumptions and attitudes[7] into their Super Egos will be affronted by the notion that there might be occasions when 'real managers' do not take all decisions themselves and actually allow others to be part of the decision-making process. However, by the word 'subordinates' I do not mean every Tom, Dick or Harriet in the organisation, but only the immediate subordinate team responsible to the manager. For example, the relevant subordinate team for the managing director would consist only of his fellow directors and not the middle management of the organisation. For the manager of a plant, the relevant subordinate team might be his first line supervisors, but certainly not every member of the shop floor.

In this context, there is a number of 'typical' styles of leadership behaviour that have traditionally been used by winning managers. Against each of the styles I have listed some examples of the typical sorts of behaviour that go with them:

STYLES OF LEADERSHIP

STYLES	BEHAVIOUR
	(manager centred)
	ruling
autocratic	telling
	manipulating
manipulative	selling
	persuading
	consulting
participative[8]	participating
	joining
	deferring
laissez faire	avoiding
	abdicating
	(team centred)

An examination of the nature of each of the 'typical' styles of management will show that, while each has its uses in meeting the particular requirements of given managerial situations, single-minded use of any one of them will not achieve the required results. The message for you is that flexibility and versatility are the hallmarks of success in the field of leadership and that inflexibility is the mark of the loser.

Let us look at the four typical styles of leadership in the listing above. Of course, for the sake of argument and description, they are idealised. Most managers' styles will approximate around the ideal types, but the ideas will be much the same. Against each, following the methods of Lewis B. Sappington and C. G. Browne,[9] I have identified the sort of communication pattern that characterises each of the styles.

Autocratic management

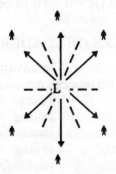

In this style the manager determines all policy and action without reference to other people. As you will see from the communication map above, there is a one-way flow of information L–>s from leader to subordinate, with information being issued bit by bit. There is no room in this style for questioning of the leader's directions either on policy or on the way policy is to be achieved. In fact, the bit-by-bit flow of information makes it unlikely that subordinates will be able to establish a big enough picture of the overall task of the team to be able to formulate a view on policy. This is exacerbated by the fact that team members are usually dealt with as isolated individuals, with no encouragement or perceived need for them to communicate other than with the leader, who decides who does what and how it is to be done.

This is a very common picture of idealised management style in the minds of most managers and will have wormed its way into many Super Egos to become the pattern of how management ought to be. As Robert McMurry[10] points out in his article, 'The case for benevolent autocracy', this is the style with which most hard-driving top managers feel most comfortable. It fits the needs of their strong Id drives that combine with the Super Ego to make up the sort of autocratic personality that Norman Dixon[11] argues often pushes its way to the top of organisations. However, like the other styles outlined above, it has drawbacks when used as the only style in the manager's repertoire.

The autocratic management style is most suitable for 'one-off' contingencies, when no other style is appropriate. When there is urgent need for action, particularly if there is danger to individuals or the organisation, then it is particularly appropriate: action is essential and the leader needs to set it in motion quickly. As we have seen from the inhibiting effects of groups on behaviour, emergencies need the sort of firm and immediate response that can only come from one person taking charge and directing action. Used as the major theme of one's management style, however, it has considerable problems.

The autocratic style is most useful to the manager who faces the vital task of overhauling traditional patterns with no team behind him. To take a controversial example, in 1979 Margaret Thatcher became British Prime Minister. She led a party that was deeply divided. On one hand, there were the new breed Tories, who shared her desire for an economic and social revolution in Britain. On the other, there remained a powerful and influential residue of the old Tory party who mistrusted change and were drawn towards the social democratic consensus[12] that had provided the framework for British politics since 1945. Read any accounts of Lady Thatcher's tenure of office as Prime Minister. You will see that, in her attempt to form and manage a cabinet that could unite her party, she chose a clearly autocratic style of leadership. Only by doing this could she have achieved success in transforming the face of British society.

The Thatcher example, however, shows the dangers of the autocratic style when it continues to be used over a prolonged period. By its nature, it stunts the growth of subordinates. Thus when the leader has to stand aside, as all managers do in time, there is no successor.

Hicks and Gullett[13] point out that one of the characteristics of the autocratic style is that its proponents categorise their subordinates as 'good' or 'bad', as 'in' or 'out, as 'one of us' or 'not one of us'. The characteristic conforms to Eric Berne's analysis[14] that subordinates seek to appease the Parent figure. The darker side of this stunted leader/subordinate relationship, however, is that subordinates become increasingly resentful about the suppression of the needs of their Ids. It produces cowed and alienated subordinates who mutter behind the leader's back and are only too willing to join in his or her destruction once the leader's power begins to crumble.

No case study better exemplifies the dangers of the autocratic management style continued over time than the experience of the last years of Thatcher's premiership. A style that was appropriate and arguably necessary under the conditions of her early cabinets became unnecessary as the Tory old guard gave way to new men who shared her vision. However, the leader did not change her style. Cut off by the one-way flow of information that accompanies a leadership style that punishes questionings as recalcitrance, there was no one who could tell her that resentment against her was making her a liability to her party. History records how she was ousted from office. She appeared to be genuinely shocked by the resentment against her amongst her colleagues. To the end, Margaret Thatcher could not see that the management style that had been necessary to get the job done in the early years had shielded her from the knowledge that her political product was no longer a success in the electoral market place. As late as January 1990, Hugo Young[15] quotes her as telling journalists that 'the very leadership style which you criticise has in fact done a very great deal for Britain.'

Personal Experience Exercise

$ Can you think of an example from your own organisation of a decision that had to be made autocratically?

$ Can you identify a manager whom you know, who nearly always uses an autocratic style of management?

$ What is the reaction to this manager of his subordinates? Is it positive or negative?

Participative management

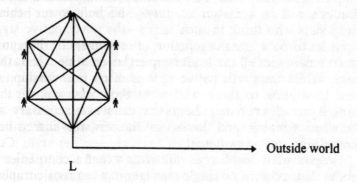

The participative management style differs sharply from the autocratic style. Rather than emphasising the role of the leader as policy-maker and arbiter of how policy is to be implemented, it looks to the team as the source of decision-making and implementation.

You will note that the communication map for this style

of leadership differs markedly from the previous one. Instead of a one-way flow of information from leader to subordinate, the style is characterised by a free flow of information shared by the team as a whole. You will note also the position of the leader in this style of management. His function is that of a coordinator and he joins the team much as an ordinary team member, with special responsibilities for facilitation and outward communication.

Under this style of leadership the whole team is responsible for all aspects of the decision-making process, including the division of labour within the team. There is no question of the imposition of a 'party line' on members: all are expected to participate and dissension is seen as positive. Once the team has made its decision, however, all team members are expected to back that decision and to make it work.

This style of leadership is, of course, anathema to the overbearing autocrat of McMurry's 'benevolent autocracy'. To those whose Ids demand their own way at once it represents instant frustration. For the Super Ego that sees leadership as some holy trust that demands the imposition of the leader's will as a matter of duty—and believe me, there are losers who think in such terms—the participative style appears to be a gross dereliction of responsibility. For you, in common with all the leadership styles identified, it has its uses. While the participative style is often time-consuming and frustrating to those who want their way and want it now, it provides two ingredients that can make the difference between winning and losing in the organisation game: *knowledge* and *commitment*.

Despite what McMurry's autocrats would like to believe about their powers, no single manager in a modern, complex organisation can expect to have sufficient knowledge to make winning decisions. The difficulty is not only associated with limited access to facts; it also concerns the need to view complex problems from a variety of perspectives. Jürgen Habermas[16] argues that technology is consciousness-forming, that is to say that exposure to certain sorts of training in a technical skill, followed by immersion in the application of that skill, gives an individual a particular way of looking at problems. From our own experience we all know that engineers seem to have a different way of thinking from accountants, who look at their world differently from marketing people. Studies of such a seemingly homogeneous profession as the Army show that, even there, infantry generals have a different perspective from cavalrymen or logisticians.[17]

Again, no one manager can have access to all the different perspectives that the variety of skills found in modern organisations can bring to bear on problems. As we have seen, autocratic styles of leadership result in the leader imposing his vision on the team. A major strength of the participative style of decision-making, however, is that it stimulates individuals to improve the problem-solving process. This should not be taken as advocating constant rounds of meetings to get things done. Formal meetings, particularly if they take place on a regular basis, usually end up with people finding things to bring to them in order to be seen to be participating. Rather, the participative leadership style is available to the winning manager to bring a depth of knowledge and a variety of perspectives to decision-making.

The second benefit of the participative style is that it gains the commitment of those involved. Autocratic managers will often deny the need for commitment from their subordinates; some may even regard it as an admission of weakness. They favour reliance upon orders backed by discipline to gain compliance. However, a recurrent theme in managerial life is the need to make people agree to perform difficult tasks. This is a particular problem for the manager who is responsible for leading a team over whom he has little or no power. When, for example, the manager has to gain the commitment of others who share his position on the lateral arms of the organisational cross, no amount of autocratic bullying will force people to relinquish what they perceive to be their best interests or the interests that they represent in the organisation.

On the other hand, the participative style seems to have an almost magic power to gain commitment and positive results, often against the odds. It appears that when people

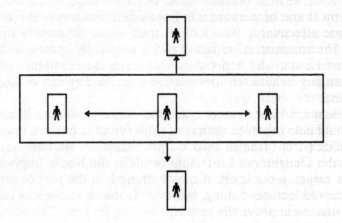

are included in a difficult or uncomfortable decision or are given the opportunity to say their piece, they have a moral stake in making the decision work. Once the decision is 'theirs'—of them, by them and for them—they are likely to be committed to its success.

This idea may be anathema to many managers whose Super Egos have been stuffed with rules which stress the macho value of autocracy and manipulation. Let me offer you the results of three examples—one experiment and two case studies—which illustrate the power and effectiveness of the participative style when other methods would have failed.

During the Second World War the USA suffered a meat shortage. Most of the strapping young lads of the American Mid West, who would otherwise have been raising grain crops to feed beasts for the meat market, were in Europe fighting my cousins. The US government was aware that the problem could be solved if the American housewife could be persuaded to change her culinary habits. There was enough meat available; the problem was that parts of animals that have traditionally featured in European cuisine—liver, kidneys, tongue, heart, intestines, brains and so on—were never served at the American table. How could Americans be weaned off their exclusive taste for the prime cuts of meat and be persuaded to use the stock of available meat more effectively?

The administration called on the help of the psychologist, Kurt Lewin, who had carried out research into methods of changing behaviour. Lewin set up an experiment to determine the best way for the government to convey its message.[18] He targeted influential women's groups which would help promote changes in culinary behaviour: women's guilds, parent-teacher associations, church groups and lodges of the Daughters of the American Revolution. He divided his target groups, arbitrarily into two. Those on one list received lectures from a nutritional expert on the problem of the meat shortage and the use of offal as a nutritious alternative. Groups on the other list were invited to meet to discuss the problem. In the latter case, the nutritional expert was present but acted only in the role of coordinator and adviser, stating the problem and giving technical advice when invited to do so. At the end of each session group members were given a list of recipes involving the use of offal and were invited to try them. After six months Lewin contacted those who had attended the sessions to discover their impact on eating habits.

The results demonstrated the power of the participative style of leadership. Of those women who had attended lecture sessions where they were told what the problem was and how it could be solved, with little or no opportunity for input, only three per cent tried one of the recipes during the six-month period. On the other hand, those who had attended the participative sessions, where they were encouraged to define the problem and find a solution for themselves, 32 per cent were motivated to try the recipes. It could be argued that 32 per cent is still a small change in behaviour; however, it should be noted that this was the result of one session that was not in the context of an organisation where it would be backed up by other support. Nevertheless, it represented a tenfold increase in the behavioural change sought by Lewin and the US government.

It may come as a surprise to most civilians to know that the value of participative leadership styles has long been recognised in the British Army. Of course it is not customary, in the middle of an engagement, to ask the enemy to stop firing while there is a general discussion as to the merits of a right- or left-flanking assault. Nevertheless, a commander who did not call for suggestions from his immediate subordinates would be unusual and probably not likely to live long on the battle field. Just like any large civilian organisation, the British Army requires quality decisions backed by strong commitment. Here is one example of the use of participative leadership style being used by the Army to make a difficult decision. It concerns the fate of an old and proud Scottish infantry regiment confronting extinction in the face of defence cuts.

Unlike other armies, the British Army does not have a Corps of Infantry. Its infantry regiments are independent units, who recruit their soldiers from a small local area and have histories dating back to before the Restoration of the monarchy in the seventeenth century.[19] In 1967, a reduction in the number of infantry regiments meant that the Cameronians, the junior regiment of Scottish Lowland infantry, had to go. The choice was an amalgamation with another Lowland regiment, or complete disbandment, with a dispersal of its members to the other Scottish regiments. The Ministry of Defence could have imposed one or other solution on the regiment; however, the results of the wrong decision could have proved disastrous for the Army. The Cameronians were not easy to integrate, either in an amalgamation or individually. Their tribal loyalty was even fiercer than that of other British regiments. They were raised to put down the seventeenth century Catholic rising in the West of Scotland and their enlisted ranks continued to be drawn from the notoriously militant Protestant working class of Glasgow. These were men whose traditional loyalties could only be ignored with peril. Amalgamation with an Edinburgh-based regiment, with the likelihood of ex-Cameronians serving under Catholic officers, would have transformed two good fighting battalions into one divided

unit made ineffective by internal squabbling. Enforced disbandment would have fomented widespread discontent
among ex-Cameronians dispersed to other parts of the
infantry.

The British Defence Ministry fell back on participative
leadership for the decision. Every serving Cameronian, from
private soldier to general, was given a vote on the choice—
amalgamation or disbandment. There was an overwhelming
vote for disbandment and the regiment accepted its fate
with dignity.

In 1921, the British government under the premiership of
David Lloyd-George met the representatives of the Irish
independence movement with the aim of finding the terms
and conditions on which the British should cease to rule
Ireland after the best part of a thousand years. After a
bitter war between the British administration and the Irish
Republican Army it was clear that independence of some
sort was necessary to end the conflict. One of the leaders of
the Irish delegation was Michael Collins, a staunch Republican who had fought the British Army and had a price of
£10,000 on his head for the killings in which he had been
involved during the troubles.[20]

The Southern Irish had voted for a republic, to include
the North, totally cut off from King and Commonwealth.
Their representatives had been sent to negotiate for this.
The British, however, wanted Ireland to have limited independence, confined to local, domestic matters. The talks
thrashed out point for point the demands of the two sides.
At the end of two months the best deal that the Irish could
extract from Lloyd-George was dominion status for Ireland,
with the King as head of state and the Protestant North to
decide for itself at a later date as to whether it was to join
the Catholic South. The alternative was a resumption of the
war with the British.

Collins was not afraid of war. He knew that the choice
was war with the British or civil war with a minority of the
South of Ireland who would never accept the compromise
that he had extracted. Together with the other members of
the Irish delegation he signed the agreement that was to

form a basis for a treaty granting Ireland independence within the Commonwealth, on the same terms as Canada. Despite his intense republican sentiments, on his return to Ireland he was a leading advocate of the treaty and fought and died in the civil war against those who would not accept its terms. Historians have argued about Collins's motives. Part of his steadfastness to the treaty was the fact that he was an honourable man who could not go back on what he saw as his word. However, the depth of his commitment to the treaty, a compromise of the principles he had fought for earlier, can only be explained as a commitment to something that he had helped to create and which, by being part of its creation, he had to make work.

Personal Experience Exercise
$ Can you think of a decision that would have been improved had more people been involved in its making?
$ Can you think of a decision that you have made that would have been better received by your subordinates if they had been involved in its making?

Laissez faire management

At first glance the laissez faire leadership style may seem to have little place in your repertoire. It can be summarised as a style where the manager abdicates responsibility and leaves his subordinates alone to 'do their own thing'. The laissez faire manager has little participation in the work of the team. He will supply information when it is needed, but subordinates have to come to him. Unlike other styles we have discussed, this management style is highly reactive, deferring action until the point is reached when the manager has to intervene.

Clearly, a manager who uses this style as his consistent response to his job is not likely to achieve results. In reality, however, many managers operate in this style in the hope

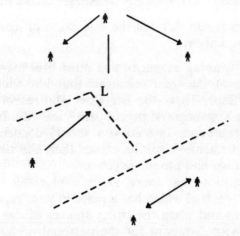

that it just might work for them. On the other hand, when used sparingly, under the right circumstances, it has its value, along with the other styles discussed above.

Both McMurry's autocratic leaders and those new to the art of management share a vision of their role as one that requires them to have an opinion of everything about them and to get involved in every activity, however small, that falls within their domain. You, however, will be able to suppress the urges of your Id to control unimportant things. You can ignore the crap Super Ego rule that emphasises the importance of immediate action all the time and will intervene only when absolutely necessary.

Personal Experience Exercise

$ Have you ever felt that you had to intervene to make a decision when, if you had stood back from it, matters would have resolved themselves with less trouble?

$ Can you think of an example when someone around you has made more work by getting involved too early, rather than waiting to see what developed?

A CASE STUDY IN LEADERSHIP STYLES

Two themes run through the discussion of leadership styles as outlined above.

- As a winning manager you must break away from the image of the 'real manager' that has been planted in your Super Ego—the Big Boss who resembles Norman Dixon's managerial psychopath[21] and McMurry's benevolent autocrat. Instead you should concentrate on the need to achieve results rather than the need to satisfy your own and others' psyches.
- The notion that there exists a plurality of leadership styles, each of which has a place in your repertoire, to be used as and when the circumstances of the moment dictate, with disregard for the personal preferences of the manager for a given style.

In terms of the choice of an ongoing style of management, I believe that there is a time and a place for each style, which coincides with the phases of project maturity that we have already discussed. My purpose here is to present some experimental evidence as to the effects of the three leadership styles so far discussed upon the behaviour of work teams.

Ralph White and Gordon Lippitt were two research students working with Kurt Lewin.[22] In order to test the effects of different managerial styles, they took vacation jobs in a youth club, where they volunteered to run the model-making activity. Each day, for a period of two weeks, groups of children were assigned to White and Lippitt who were responsible for supervising them while they went about the task of building model ships, aeroplanes and so on. The activity remained the same, but the style in which the researchers managed each group of children differed according to a carefully conceived plan.

One group was assembled and told what models were to be made and how this was to be done. No deviation from the supervisors' plans was allowed and a strict regime of work was insisted upon and enforced. With a second set of children, the researchers began the session with a discussion on what should be made and how the work was to be carried out. The adults provided information as to what was possible and the best methods of achieving the children's chosen designs and joined in the process, encouraging and helping. With a third set of children White and Lippitt merely announced that this was the model-making activity and that the children were expected to make models. They were shown the available materials and equipment and left to get on with the task. With these, the adults showed little interest but confined themselves to answering questions, if asked. These three different approaches clearly represented the autocratic, the participative and the laissez faire styles of leadership respectively.

The researchers carefully watched and documented the behaviour of each group of children. Their findings are of great importance to a winning manager who needs the cooperation and assistance of others to shift product quickly and with as little pain and effort as possible. Two observations are particularly relevant. First, the behaviour of the little workers when White and Lippitt absented themselves, but continued to observe their charges, unseen. In the case of both the autocratically and the laissez faire-managed children, work rates fell to one third of the level of when the adult supervisors were present. On the other hand, those who were managed by the participative style of leadership continued with their tasks, despite the absence of supervision. For those managers who remain unconvinced as to the need to buy their subordinates' souls, here is evidence that can be translated into practical terms. Supervision is expensive and cannot be all-seeing. Here we see the participative style overcoming this limitation by providing motivation for those managed by it to continue to shift product, supervised by themselves alone.

Perhaps the most interesting finding of the experiment, however, related to the attitude of the children to the models they had made. White and Lippitt observed their behaviour when they were told to down tools at the end of the camp. The children from the laissez faire groups showed a complete lack of interest in the models that they had spent two weeks making. This contrasted with the behaviour of the participative group who, almost to a boy and girl, picked up their models to take home to show Mom and Dad. Their models were clearly a part of themselves and they took a pride in them. The really telling behaviour, however, was that of the autocratically managed groups. When the end of the modelling sessions was announced, these children set about destroying their work of a fortnight. The models were hurled to the floor and the children made a ritualistic game from their destruction. The models had become a symbol of frustration, anger and alienation that the autocratic style of management had engendered in them. Again, if you mean to become a winning manager, there is a clear message. You need not merely compliance but the active participation of others if you are to succeed. Managerial styles that risk engendering the alienation of those on whom you rely to shift product may follow the losers' agenda of satisfying the dictates of the managers' psyche, but have no place in a strategy for winning.

Which style would you use?

The controlling phase is right for the laissez faire manager. He will leave people alone to get on with the job, intervening only when necessary. Here is where you can use Clausewitz's *simple and lazy* man.

The motivating phase is where the participative style comes into its own. The natural instincts of those with a democratic style are to invite participation and to concentrate on Adair's second element of effective leadership, team maintenance, getting the group working together to carry out the task in the best possible way with their souls bought by the power of group involvement.

The planning phase can afford the autocratic style. When the task is being set up, it requires the managerial stamp. Adair's first element of effective management, the task, is all-important. The people who are to perform it, and their needs, come later. The team is not yet involved. Here is a

Project Life Cycle

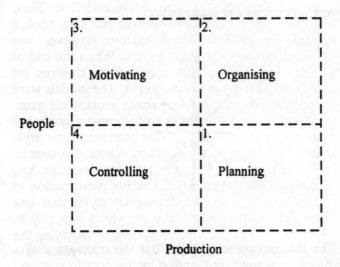

Production

job for Clausewitz's *shrewd and hard-working* manager. He will beaver away getting the system running correctly before people are allowed to get their hands on it.

But what about the organising phase? What style of leadership is required there? We know from Blake and Mouton that this needs someone who realises the importance of making sure that both the production system and the people involved fit well together. This phase needs a style of management that concentrates on Adair's third element: the individual needs of the people who work for you. It needs a leadership style that concentrates on buying the souls of the individual team members by showing them, as individuals, what is in it for them.

Conventional leadership theory does not offer a style that meets this requirement. I therefore offer you a new one. The top right-hand corner of the project life cycle needs a manager who knows how to buy the souls of those who are to perform tasks on his behalf. The leadership style of this new, winning manager is the manipulative style.

MANIPULATIVE MANAGEMENT

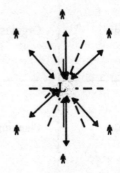

This is like the autocratic style in that the manager determines all policy himself, but unlike his autocratic counterpart, he sees the need for some involvement by his team. This time, therefore, the communication map documents a two-way flow of information L<->s between leader and subordinate. The manipulative style uses this two-way flow in two ways.

First, at a practical level, the manager will use it to gain facts that he might otherwise not have at his grasp. To this extent, the potential weakness of the autocratic style's reliance on one person—the manager—having a monopoly of ideas and knowledge is avoided by drawing on the advice of the team as individuals. The manipulative element of the style derives from the manager's ability to use this information to his political advantage.

By seeming to be drawn into the management process by the leader, each team member is made to feel important and valued as a colleague. Even though the manager will ensure that his agenda will be pursued, he will emphasise the importance of each individual's contribution to the formation of policy and the shifting of product. However, the style of communication deals with subordinates as individuals and allows them little scope for acting together in a way similar to but more subtle than autocratic management. By dealing with his subordinates one by one and hinting at a special personal relationship, perhaps even in a pact against others, the manipulative manager shows each individual how he or she can best succeed by doing what he wants. He uses personal contact to find the special needs that motivate each individual. He then buys their loyalty and their compliance—their souls—while taking the opportunity to sell his policy and his means of achieving it. If he applies the principles of Chapter Six he will soon find that the rewarding of compliant behaviour will make the business of getting his way with his subordinates a matter of routine.

As with the autocratic style, there is little likelihood that subordinates will be able to construct a sufficiently detailed picture of the overall task to challenge his dominion. Unlike the autocratic style, which usually breeds resentment among subordinates, manipulative management removes the need for individuals to revolt as they each have a satisfactory communication channel with the manager. Nevertheless, a sensible degree of paranoia is required to ensure that subordinates' souls remain bought.

While no managerial style is appropriate for all contingencies, manipulative management can be used as the major style of decision-making and implementation. Admittedly, it takes time and effort. However, once in place, continued positive reinforcement of good compliant behaviour will minimise the time spent on managerial effort.

The openly cynical approach of the manipulative style may mean that you will have to work on reprogramming your Super Ego. It is interesting that, while textbooks on management devote much space to the first three leadership styles discussed above, no mention is made of the manipulative approach. It is clear that conventional management morality has little place for a manipulative style in its teaching. Again, we have seen the danger of the Super Ego's impatience with the need to take time and trouble in dealing with the sometimes laborious business of managing people.

You may resent the time spent on manipulation when you can see your goal and are impatient of others' lack of vision. To this loser's approach I would quote the late Basil Liddell Hart writing on military strategy, 'The longest way round is often the shortest way home'.[23]

Personal Experience Exercise
$ Can you think of an occasion when a manipulative style would have obtained the best results from people about you?

Children and manipulative management

How would a manipulative manager manage the children in the model-making exercise of White and Lippitt?

He would begin by ensuring that the children were clear about his desired outcomes for the exercise—namely, to produce 12 models with minimum faults within a set period of time. Realising that he could only achieve his aims through the willing cooperation of others, he would cultivate an intimately dependent relationship with each one, establishing what made them tick and what motivated them. As the project progressed he would feed these motivational needs—for example, self-importance, achievement, respect, attention, jelly beans.

Aware that confrontation and bossiness are inimical to productivity, he would try to develop a friendly and dynamic atmosphere in order to boost productivity.

Unlike his autocratic counterpart, he is therefore likely to avoid the destructive influence of groups and ensure that respect for his leadership is maintained.

He would also allow his team to achieve their goals in their own way. This conforms to Clausewitz's portrayal of the shrewd and lazy manager. Delegation of the boring but necessary tasks would be given to his right-hand boy or girl, he or she conforming to Clausewitz's shrewd and hard-working manager. All desired behaviour would be rewarded and punishment would be issued only when absolutely necessary. Results? Positive.

WINNING THE ORGANISATION GAME

At the beginning of this book I introduced you to a real winner in the organisation game—the shrewd but lazy manager. This is the Super Manager who will inherit the managerial world, for he cannot be beaten by the organisational system or its inhabitants. He represents the model for the winning manager, never faltering from the Thirteen Winner's Commandments:

1 *Me first. Nobody else will put your interests before theirs*
Never shy away from following the dictates of self-interest. This is the only way to attain power in the organisation and to avoid others about you dumping their agenda on you.

2 *There are no absolute rules. Other people's ideas of right and wrong do not apply to you*
Organisations and, more to the point, the people in them, are a breeding ground for all sorts of crap rules and misplaced loyalties that will get in your way if you let them. The only way to be a winner is to reject all of them and make your own.

3 *The organisation is there to serve your interests, not the other way round*
The organisation will be only too ready to ditch you when you no longer serve its interests. Do not have any qualms about exploiting it to get what you want, while you still can. If in doubt, ask George Bush, Mikhail Gorbachev or any of yesterday's winners.

4 *You are on your own. Nobody is going to help you become a winner*
Remember that the others around you are governed by their own self-interest; they have a stake in stopping you from

winning. Be prepared to help them and encourage others, but only when it serves to further your interests.

5 *Be paranoic. Watch out, the bastards* are *out to get you*
Not only is the self-interest of others a threat to you, the psyche of even the losers around you can jeopardise your success. People will be only too glad to see you become a loser.

6 *Suck up to those who matter and suck up well. Identify the key people in the system who will help you*
Do not worry about being loyal to your peers. You need to identify those who matter in the organisation and to see that you are well thought of and likely to be helped and protected on your path to winning. Find a patron who will look after your interests.

7 *Say one thing and do another. You need to pay lip-service to the organisation's cherished notion of how things should be done*
Be cynical. Who really cares about the organisation and its symbols? But the winner cannot afford to be open about his cynicism. If the organisation thinks that TQM is God's gift to management, then act accordingly in public and laugh up your sleeve at its stupidity.

8 *Be a team-player, but make sure you beat your fellow team members*
Organisations stress team work and group loyalty. But we have seen what these can do to the manager's resolve to win. Go through the motions of being a good team-player, but be ready to ditch the team and its members when the time suits you.

9 *Remember that the truth is not always to your advantage. Those who control your future do not necessarily want to hear the bad news*
Tell your superiors what they want to hear. Always bring them solutions rather than problems, even when those solu-

tions belong to others. Convince them that the good ideas come from you, not the losers who surround you.

10 *Manipulate the facts to suit your interests. Even when things are bad you should come up smelling of roses*
In your dealings with your superiors, remember that the way you present information will have an effect upon their view of you. You will often be the first there with a story. You may be lucky enough to be the only one. Always bear in mind your need to be seen in a positive light. Omission or enhancement of the facts can usually help to make a good impression on those who matter. The carefully constructed lie can often be invaluable.

11 *Get your retaliation in first. When there is blood on the organisation's carpet, make sure it's not yours*
Do not lose an opportunity to do your rivals down. Look for opportunities to undermine their credibility in the eyes of your superiors. Think how you can use your responsibilities to make the attainment of their goals impossible and then make sure they get the blame when things go wrong.

12 *Blow your own trumpet—or better still, get someone else to do it for you*
Make sure that your contribution to the organisation does not go unnoticed. Look for opportunities to have your name associated with the positive things that happen. Better still, try to ensure that this association is talked about by the others around you, so that it becomes part of the organisation's culture.

13 *Dominate your environment or it will dominate you*
You need to be driven by the will to win. This means that you must be determined to be proactive in shaping the events around you. If you fail to be proactive in imposing your will on others, they will impose their will on you and you will end up a loser.

Are you a winning manager? Do you have the drive, initiative and, above all, the will, to become a Super Manager—one who stands above the petty concerns of the organisation and its inhabitants? While reading this book is a step in the right direction, you will only gain power over your life if you apply the lesson it contains.

First and foremost, you need to be clear about what you want from the organisation. For the lucky few, it is a source of power in the generally understood meaning of that term. Their place in the organisation gives them the wherewithal to dominate their environment by dint of the wealth and status that they derive from their position. For most organisation members, power is strictly limited by the nature of the organisation they inhabit. Most losers, however, are so passive that they become victims of the organisation, lacking control over their lives and having their careers determined by others. You must, therefore, decide what you want from your job before pursuing this goal relentlessly and ruthlessly.

This determination requires an objective, detached and cynical approach, one based upon results rather than form and style, as is so often the case in modern organisations. When confronted with a task you must ask yourself, 'What is the minimum I must do in order to achieve the required outcome I want?' The niceties of 'management as an art form' as exemplified by the latest fads, such as Total Quality Management or the concerns of the ethics industry for socially responsible management, are merely traps to deflect the loser. For you, the organisation, its activities and its members are only a means to one end—getting what you want out of the system; fulfilling your own personal, private and very selfish agenda.

Of course you have to live in an organisational world made up of rules. There are the formal rules of what the organisation will tolerate as acceptable ways of doing things. There are also the informal rules that the cultures of all organisations expect their members to follow. You, the shrewd but lazy Super Manager, are the one who sees these rules for what they are. It may be necessary to obey some of them. In public, of course, you will proclaim that everyone should obey them and will express your admiration for the person who wrote them. But privately you will dismiss them as obstacles between you and your goals. You must not allow your Super Ego to take them on board so that they become a hindrance to your achieving a domination of your managerial world. Quietly and secretly, you must be prepared to cheat on these rules to gain advantage within the organisational system.

There are other ways in which you can use the organisation to your advantage.

- Take advantage of any opportunities to learn skills that are transferable inside and outside the organisation.
- Once you have obtained training from the organisation, you can make yourself useful to other parts of the bureaucracy.
- You will stay in the organisation only while it offers you advantages; once it has ceased to do so you will go elsewhere for higher rewards.
- You will use your experience as a bargaining tool for better jobs.

The process of working with others in the organisation is a vital one. As we have seen, management is about getting other people to do things. It follows from this that you will become a winning manager by learning to manipulate others so that they come to do your will, rather than impose their will upon you. Other people in the organisation must be seen only as vehicles for the achievement of your aims. While you must rely upon influence to get your way with your superiors, you need even more subtle ways with those who must help you to succeed—your subordinates. You must identify the rewards that win their compliance and then use them to buy their souls, so that they act, automatically, in your interest.

All this will not buy you friends amongst your colleagues. But you never really had friends amongst your colleagues anyway. Your peers are of two sorts. A few will be your rivals. They are in direct competition with you for power in the organisation. They are likely to succeed and their success is equally likely to be your failure. The majority will be losers. Given what we have seen of the normal human propensity to impose the discipline of the group upon its members, they will try, both consciously and unconsciously, to impose their losers' mentality and culture upon you. While you should respect and watch out for the former, you can only despise the latter. The friendship of either category is not worthy of you, the would-be Super Manager, who must stand above the primitive pull of the group and its norms. You have your own winning agenda which sets you apart from others around you.

Throughout this book I have been at pains to show how organisations and the people within them are, inherently, at odds with the needs of the sort of manager who has the innate desire to use his creativity, initiative and will to stand above the mass of his peers and dominate his environment. The perspective of this book is deliberately anti-organisational, in that it seeks to show you the barriers that the social system of the organisation sets up against your inner drives. If you like, it is an appeal to the individualism of the individual manager.

Those of you who are blessed with insight will look beyond this concentration on the needs of the individual to see the benefit that can accrue to organisations that encourage the development of a style of management which throws off the hindering shackles of conventional teaching. It is true that I speak to you, the individual manager, and invite you to centre your managerial world upon yourself, rather than on and in the organisation. But in doing so you must become a better manager. The paradox is that the more you approximate to the winning Super Manager that is advocated in this book—freed from the constraints of the organisation and its social system—the greater becomes your use to the organisation.

You, as a winning manager, may be selfish and self-centred, but you need the organisation in which to manage. You may have defined your goals in your own terms, but unless they take into account the need to achieve organisational objectives, you will fail. However, your self-centredness will ensure that you use your manipulative skills so as not to fail. And here is the point of coincidence between the two, seemingly opposed, sets of needs—those of the organisation and of the individual. By freeing yourself from the constraints that organisations impose upon their members, you become better able to manage the business of your organisation. Freed from the loyalties and the crap rules that constrain others, and having chosen your own path, you can get on with being a winning manager. As a result, both you and your organisation become winners in the organisation game. Enjoy winning!

Notes and References

CHAPTER ONE: THE ORGANISATION GAME

1 Thompson, A. and Strickland, A. (1990). *Strategic Management: Concepts and Cases*, Homewood: Irwin.
2 Potter, S. (1952). *One-Upmanship*, Harmondsworth: Penguin.
3 Berne, E. (1964). *Games People Play*, Harmondsworth: Penguin.
4 Whyte, W. H. (1953). *The Organisation Man*, New York: Simon & Schuster.
5 Rapoport, A. (ed.) (1968). *Carl von Clausewitz on War*, Harmondsworth: Penguin.
6 See Chapter Six: Buying Souls.
7 See Chapter Two: The Enemy Within.
8 See Chapter Two: The Enemy Within.
9 Dixon, N. (1987). *Our Own Worst Enemy*, London: Futura.
10 *Ibid*.
11 Lock, D. and Farrow, N. (eds.) (1983). *The Complete Manager*, Aldershot: Gower.
12 Nietzsche, F. (1886). *Beyond Good and Evil*, trs. W. Kaufmann (1966), New York: Vintage.
13 Perrow, C. (1972). 'Technology, Organisations and Environment: a Cautionary Note'. Paper presented to the British Sociological Association.
14 My colleague, Miss Eleanor Shaw of the University of Glasgow, explains 'organisational culture' very succinctly as 'the way we do things around here'.
15 Weber, M. (1930). *The Protestant Ethic and the Spirit of Capitalism*, trs. T. Parson, London: Unwin.
16 Taylor, F. (1947). *Scientific Management*, New York: Harper & Row.
17 French proverb—'*Le mieux est l'ennemi du bien*', in Grant, G. (1923). *Dictionary of Foreign and Classical Quotations*, Edinburgh: Grant.
18 See Chapter Two: The Enemy Within.

CHAPTER TWO: THE ENEMY WITHIN

1 Berne, E. (1964). *Games People Play*, Harmondsworth: Penguin.
2 Dixon, N. (1987). *Our Own Worst Enemy*, London: Futura.
3 *Ibid*.

4   See Chapter Three: Joined Up Enemies.
5   Berne, E., *op. cit.*
6   Dixon, N. *op. cit.*
7   Bannister, D. (1966). 'Psychology as an Exercise in Paradox', in *Bulletin of the British Psychological Society*, No. 19.
8   See Chapter Six: Buying Souls.
9   'Malicious enjoyment of others' misfortunes'. See *The Oxford English Dictionary*.
10   Dixon, N. *op. cit.*
11   *Ibid.*
12   Nietzsche, F. (1886). *Beyond Good and Evil*, trs. W. Kaufmann (1966), New York: Vintage.
13   Habermas, J. (1971). *Towards a Rational Society*, London: Heinemann.

CHAPTER THREE: JOINED UP ENEMIES

1   Reid, J. (1994). 'Why does Scotland always demand that its heroes must fall', in *Seven Days Scotland*, No. 5.
2   Brown, J. A. C. (1954). *The Social Psychology of Industry*, Harmondsworth: Penguin.
3   Zugbach, R. G. L. von (1988). *Power and Prestige in the British Army*, Aldershot: Avebury/Gower.
4   Brown, J. A. C. *op. cit.*
5   Hastorf, A. H. and Cantril, H. (1954). 'They saw a Game: a Case Study', in *Journal of Abnormal and Social Psychology*, No. 49.
6   Gilbert, G. M. (1951). 'Stereotype Persistence and Change among College Students', in *Journal of Abnormal and Social Psychology*, No. 46.
7   Dixon, N. (1976). *On the Psychology of Military Incompetence*, London: Jonathan Cape.
8   Quinn, J. B. *et al.* (1988). *The Strategy Process*, Englewood Cliffs: Prentice Hall.
9   Sherif, M. (1936). *The Psychology of Norms*, New York: Harper.
10   Allport, F. H. (1924). *Social Psychology*, Boston: Houghton Mifflin.
11   This notion of 'social facilitation' has been instrumental in the development of the technique of 'brainstorming' whereby ideas are generated by a group who are encouraged to let their imaginations run free.
12   Zajonc, R. B. (1965). 'Social Facilitation', in *Science*, vol. 149.
13   *Ibid.*
14   Larsson, K. (1956). *Conditioning and Sexual Behaviour*, Stockholm: Almquist & Wiksell.
15   Zajonc, R. B., *op. cit.*
16   Latané, B. and Darley, J. (1968). 'Group Inhibition of Bystander Intervention in Emergencies', in *Journal of Personality and Social Psychology*, vol. 10.

17 Sealy, A. P. (1976). 'The LSE Jury Project Report No. 1', London: LSE.
18 Asch, S. (1955). 'Opinions and Social Pressure', in *Scientific American*, vol. 193.
19 Crutchfield, R. S. (1955). 'Conformity and Character', in *American Psychologist*, vol. 10.
20 Brown, J. A. C., *op. cit.*

CHAPTER FOUR: ORGANISATIONS AS YOUR ENEMY

1 Weber, M. (1964). *The Theory of Social and Economic Organisation*, New York: Free Press.
2 *Hansard*, 1968.
3 Brodie, M. B. (1967). *Fayol on Administration*, London: Lyon, Grant & Green.
4 Blau, P. M. and Schoenherr, R. A. (1971). *The Structure of Organisations*, New York: Basic Books.
5 Zugbach, R. G. L. von (1988). *Power and Prestige in the British Army*, Aldershot: Avebury/Gower.
6 Blau, P. M. and Schoenherr, R. A., *op. cit.*
7 Michels, R. (1947). *Political Parties*, New York: Free Press.
8 McGregor, I. (1986). *The Enemies Within*, London: Collins.
9 Weber, M. *op. cit.*
10 Merton, R. K. (1961). 'The Bureaucratic Personality', in Etzione, A. (ed.), *Complex Organisations: a Sociological Reader*, New York: Free Press.
11 Blau, P. M. and Schoenherr, R. A., *op. cit.*
12 Davis, A. K. (1952). 'Bureaucratic Patterns in the Navy Officer Corps', in Merton, R. K. *et al.* (eds.), *Reader in Bureaucracy*, New York: Free Press.
13 Peter, L. J. and Hull, R. (1969). *The Peter Principle*, London: Souvenir Press.
14 Dixon, N. (1987). *Our Own Worst Enemy*, London: Futura.
15 Blauner, R. (1964). *Alienation and Freedom*, Chicago: University of Chicago Press.

CHAPTER FIVE: THE WINNING AGENDA

1 Lenin, V. I. (1902). *Chto Delat?* (What has to be done?). Pamphlet.
2 Drucker, P. (1967). *The Effective Executive*, London: Pan.
3 McGregor, I. (1986). *The Enemies Within*, London: Collins.
4 MacKenzie, R. A. (1972). *The Time Trap*, New York: McGraw-Hill.
5 MacKenzie, R. A. (1970). *Managing Time at the Top*, New York: The Presidents Association.
6 Buzan, T. (1979). *Use Your Head*, London: BBC.
7 Shea, M. (1988). *Influence*, London: Century.

8 Zugbach, R. G. L. von (1988). *Power and Prestige in the British Army*, Aldershot: Avebury/Gower.
9 Machiavelli, N. (1961). *The Prince*, Harmondsworth: Penguin.
10 Kearns, D. (1976). 'Lyndon Johnson and the American Dream', in *The Atlantic Monthly*, May 1976.
11 If you do not have a personal organiser, *buy one now*. There is a tendency for losers to sneer at them. But only losers care what other losers think.
12 Dixon, N. (1976). *On the Psychology of Military Incompetence*, London: Jonathan Cape.
13 Buzan, T. *op. cit.*

CHAPTER SIX: BUYING SOULS

1 Hicks, H. G. and Gullett, C. R. (1981). *Management*, New York: McGraw-Hill.
2 See Chapter Two: The Enemy Within.
3 Dixon, N. (1976). *On the Psychology of Military Incompetence*, London: Jonathan Cape.
4 Eysenck, H. J. (1965). *Fact and Fiction in Psychology*, Harmondsworth: Penguin.
5 Foss, B. M. (1966). *New Horizons in Psychology, 1*, Harmondsworth: Penguin.
6 Wolfe, J. B. (1936). 'Effectiveness of token reward for chimpanzees', in *Comparative Psychology Monographs 12*, No. 60.
7 Huczynski, A. and Buchanan, D. (1991). *Organizational Behaviour*, Englewood Cliffs: Prentice Hall.
8 Eysenck, H. J., *op. cit.*
9 'Jumping for the Jelly Beans' (1973). Video, BBC Enterprises.
10 McGregor, D. (1960). *The Human Side of Enterprise*, New York: McGraw-Hill.
11 Beynon, H. (1975). *Working for Ford*, Wakefield: EP Publishing.
12 Huczynski, A. and Buchanan, D. *op. cit.*
13 Maslow, A. (1943). 'A Theory of Human Motivation', *in Psychological Review*, vol. 50.
14 Beynon, H., *op. cit.*
15 Herzberg, F. *et al.* (1959). *The Motivation to Work*, New York: John Wiley.

CHAPTER SEVEN: LEADERS WIN

1 Lord Slim (1962). 'Leadership', in *The Manager*, Jan. 1962.
2 Adair, J. (1968). *Training for Leadership*, London: Macdonald.
3 Adair sees this process as three overlapping circles.
4 Blake, R. R. and Mouton, J. S. (1964). *The Managerial Grid*, Houston: Gulf.

5 Hershey, P. and Blanchard, K. (1977). *Management of Organisational Behaviour*, Englewood Cliffs: Prentice-Hall.

6 Hicks, H. G. and Gullett, C. R. (1981). *Management*, New York: McGraw-Hill.

7 See Chapter Six: Buying Souls.

8 I have deliberated the term 'democratic management', used in the conventional literature for this style. Experience has taught me that the term is offensive to many managers who misunderstand its implications for the workplace.

9 Adapted from Sappington, L. B. and Browne, C. G. (1962). 'The Skills of Creative Leadership,' in Lazer, W. and Kelly, E. J. (eds.), *Managerial Marketing: Perspectives and Viewpoints*, Homewood: Irwin. My adaptation emphasises the barriers to communication between subordinates.

10 McMurry, R. N. (1958). 'The Case for Benevolent Autocracy', in *Harvard Business Review*, January-February 1958.

11 Dixon, N. (1987). *Our Own Worst Enemy*, London: Futura.

12 For example, John Biffen, as late as 1983, proclaimed that 'We are all social democrats now'; Young, H. (1989). *One of Us*, London: Pan.

13 Hicks, H. G. and Gullett, C. R., *op. cit.*

14 Berne, E. (1964). *Games People Play*, Harmondsworth: Penguin.

15 Young, H. *op. cit.*

16 Habermas, J. (1971). *Towards a Rational Society*, London: Heinemann.

17 Zugbach, R. G. L. von (1988). *Power and Prestige in the British Army*, Aldershot: Avebury/Gower.

18 Lewin, K. (1958). 'Group Decision and Social Change', in Maccoby, E. E. *et al.* (eds.), *Readings in Social Psychology*, New York: Holt Rinehart & Hartley.

19 Zugbach, R. G. L. von, *op. cit.*

20 Younger, C. (1968). *Ireland's Civil War*, London: Fontana.

21 Dixon, N. (1987), *op. cit.*

22 White, R. and Lippitt, G. (1960). *Autocracy and Democracy*, New York: Harper & Row.

23 Liddell Hart, B. H. (1954). *Strategy: the Indirect Approach*, quoted in *War Studies*, St Albans: Metropolitan College.

Index

achievement 15, 18, 19, 22, 34, 73, 105, 109, 110, 148, 180, 185
  of results 18, 19, 136
action 6, 10, 17, 42, 53, 60–2, 75, 76, 86, 88, 94, 95, 99–101, 105, 111, 112–16, 118, 122, 127, 129, 130, 132, 140, 141, 154, 159, 162, 163, 172, 173
Adair, J. 154–6, 176, 177
Adult 28, 175
agenda, winning 77, 91, 94, 118, 186
agent, acting 14
alienation 90, 103, 144, 176
allies 21, 56, 92, 124, 138
Allport, E. 59
altruism 78
ambition 58, 71, 106
Asch, S. 62–6
authority 74, 91, 108
autokinetic effect 58

Bannister, D. 28
Bannister, R. 59
barriers 7, 15, 110, 186
bastards 1, 182
BEA 95, 96
behaviour:
  negative 29–32, 54–6, 130–4, 165
  required 5, 13, 19, 22, 30, 65, 83, 105, 110, 117, 126, 131, 133, 141, 148, 155, 159, 162, 177, 179, 184
being busy 18
Berne, E. 3, 24–6, 28, 164
Beynon, H. 138, 144, 145

Blanchard, K. 157, 158
Blake, R.R. 157, 177
Blauner, R. 90
brainwashing 1, 64
bribery 124, 138
Brown, J.A.C. 52, 68, 69
Browne, C.G. 162
Buchanan, D. 129, 139
bureaucracy 73, 74–7, 78, 80, 85, 185
bureaucratic personality 82–4
buying souls 120–51

Cantril, H. 54
career 1, 64, 86, 87, 94, 103, 114, 149, 159
  path 64, 103, 114
careerists 87
caring 14, 16, 29, 30
carrot and stick 129
character traits 55, 153
Chen, S.C. 60
Child 25, 36
Civil Service 128
Clausewitz, K. von 5–7, 176, 177, 180
collective memory 96
Collins, M. 171, 172
Commandments, the Thirteen 1, 17, 181
common sense 18, 38, 96
compliance 12, 18, 47, 67, 90, 122, 130, 136, 142, 144, 146, 152, 167, 176, 179, 185
concern:
  for people 153, 156, 158

for production 156, 159
conditioning 126
conformity 17, 28, 32, 50, 52, 53, 63, 65, 92, 112, 119
conscience 26, 36
conscientiousness 4, 44
consciousness 166
constraints 28, 35, 42, 100, 103, 107, 123, 186, 187
control 1, 2, 7, 14, 15, 24, 28, 32, 58, 60, 67, 75, 76, 85, 86, 90, 94, 97, 101–5, 110, 120, 121, 123, 125, 136–9, 147–51, 173, 182, 184
controlling 103, 159, 160, 176, 177
conventions 32
in morality 16, 17, 121
in philosophy 16
in wisdom 18, 144
corporate identity 45
crap:
ideas 152
rules 38–42, 78, 181, 187
textbooks 16
creativity 3, 29, 30, 34, 41, 84, 88
Crutchfield, R.S. 65, 66
culture 4, 18, 20, 45, 68, 92, 96, 97, 100, 101, 183, 186
cunning 51, 120
cynicism 5, 9, 79, 179, 182, 184

Darley, J. 60, 61
delegation 6, 7, 8, 14, 75, 117, 118, 171, 180
demands, unreasonable 15
deserving 15, 16, 18
determination 17, 20, 25, 56, 110, 184
discipline 16, 21, 40, 84, 167, 186
disloyalty 78, 93
Dixon, N. 24, 27, 28, 32, 56, 111, 123, 163, 174
dress 52, 69, 92
Drucker, P. 95–7

Eden, A. (Earl of Avon) 123

effectiveness 34, 51, 75, 82, 84, 86, 91, 95, 108, 168
effort 7, 10, 13, 14, 16, 18–20, 36, 43, 57, 58, 87, 88, 101, 112, 114, 116, 127, 138, 139, 148, 159, 175, 179
bargain 13, 14
minimum 19, 20
Ego 22, 24, 26–36, 38, 39, 41–3, 67, 72, 75, 81, 84, 89, 101, 112, 121, 122, 123, 129, 134, 147, 152, 154, 163, 166, 173, 174, 179, 185
states 24, 28, 30–2, 34
enemies 9, 12, 19, 20, 22–4, 27, 35, 38, 44–6, 48, 50, 52–6, 58, 60, 64, 70–4, 77, 78, 86, 95, 110, 121, 123, 170
ethics 16, 41, 184
excellence 19
experts 5
exploitation 11, 15, 18, 19, 71, 159
Eysenck, H. 133, 134

facilitation 59, 60, 150, 166
failure 3, 14, 44, 53, 87, 89, 92, 95, 96, 101, 109, 110, 123, 144, 186
Fayol, H. 74–7
fitting in 63, 75, 92, 111
Ford, H. 5
Ford Motor Company 138, 144–6
Freud, S. 22, 24, 33, 73

game, the organisation as 1–7, 9, 12, 14–22, 35, 36, 42–4, 53–5, 57, 67, 72, 77, 86, 91, 100, 101, 106, 120, 134, 138, 144, 166, 176, 181, 187
Gates, B. 5
getting your way 15, 25, 72, 76, 121, 181
getting things done 38, 41, 83, 120, 122, 156
Gilbert, G.M. 55
goals 10, 12, 15, 22, 23, 27, 48, 60, 61, 72, 78–80, 86, 94–7, 100,

105, 108, 118, 123, 136, 137, 180, 183, 185, 186
good will 15, 27, 76, 92, 112
GOYA 152
groups 11, 12, 44, 45, 47, 50–62, 64, 66–72, 95, 120, 123, 129, 150, 163, 169, 174–6, 180
  dynamics 45, 48, 52
  in-groups 69
  joining 50, 51
  norms 53, 66
  out-groups 55
  peer 9, 12, 49, 50, 52, 68, 92, 105, 144, 155, 182, 185, 186
Gullett, C.R. 159, 164

Habermas, J. 39, 166
Hansard 73
Hanson, Lord 5
Harlow, H.F. 59
Hastorf, A.H. 54
Hershey, P. 157, 158
Herzbeg, F. 135, 147, 148
Hicks, H.G. 159, 164
hierarchy 18, 47, 74, 75, 77, 86–8, 93, 97, 103, 104, 109, 110, 111, 140, 142, 143, 144, 145, 148
  of needs 140, 142, 143
Huczynski, A. 129, 139

I want 1, 22, 25, 28, 44, 106, 184
Id 22, 24–36, 41, 69, 76, 123, 134, 152, 163, 173
ideal type 80, 138
immorality 16, 17
impotence, sexual 133
influence 7, 12, 26, 28, 34, 35, 41, 44–8, 50, 53, 56–8, 62, 64, 65, 67, 94, 95, 103, 104, 106, 120, 123, 124, 136, 180, 185
  on decisions 94
  of groups 12, 44, 123, 180
inhibition 59, 60
intelligence 4, 5, 22, 38, 39, 64, 74, 93, 131, 153
interference from others 7

key sectors 112–17
knowledge 11, 43, 50, 57, 76, 80, 92, 95, 99, 100, 110, 116, 122, 128, 145, 150, 153, 154, 159, 164, 166, 167, 178

Latané, B. 60, 61
leadership 79, 88, 152–5, 161, 162, 164–7, 169–72, 174–80
  autocratic 147, 161–5, 167, 173, 175, 176, 178–80
  laissez faire 161, 172, 175, 176
  manipulative 161, 178–80, 183, 185, 187
  participative 165–71, 175, 176
  styles of 161, 162, 167, 175
legitimacy 74, 77, 78, 80
Lenin, V.I. 95
Lewin, K. 169, 174
Lippett, G. 174, 175, 180
losers:
  charter 16
  ideas 12, 121
loyalty 13, 16, 18, 19, 21, 44, 47, 54, 55, 57, 72, 73, 77, 78, 82, 84, 90, 92, 93, 110, 170, 179, 181, 182, 187

Mackenzie, R.A. 100, 102
man:
  organisation 4
  rational 26, 28, 32, 36, 50, 58, 74, 122, 134, 149
management:
  as art form 34, 81, 184
  style 12, 157, 159, 163–5, 172
manager:
  shrewd 5, 6, 8, 177, 180, 181, 184
  super 181, 184, 186
  winning 1, 2, 4–6, 8–10, 14, 16–20, 22, 24, 35, 38, 42, 46, 48, 50, 52, 53, 54, 56–8, 60, 64, 65, 72, 74, 77, 78, 90, 94, 97, 101, 117, 118, 128, 130, 138, 139, 142, 152, 154, 167, 174–6, 178, 181, 184, 185–7
manipulation 2, 12, 20, 91, 121–3

see also leadership, manipulative
Maslow, A. 140–5, 147, 148
Maxwell, R. 33
McGregor, D. 136–9
McMurry, R. 163, 166, 173, 174
meetings 14, 39, 137, 167
memos 14
Mephistopheles 120, 122, 124, 128, 135
Merton, R. 82
Michels, R. 78
monkeys, sex-starved 28
morale 40, 92, 141
morality 16, 17, 43, 121, 122, 179
own 16
Mouton, J.S. 157, 177
myths 121

National Health Service 55, 79, 80, 97
needs, lower order 143–5, 147, 148
Nietzsche, F. 36

office 6, 74–84, 86–9, 91, 103, 104, 107, 110, 164
old-timers 18
opportunism 10
O'Reilly, C. 129
organisation, modern 5, 6, 52, 73, 74, 167, 184
see also game
organisational:
cross 45, 67
journey 97, 98, 105
life 9, 11, 17–20, 100, 103
politics 90, 91

pack animal 27, 51
paranoia 1, 5, 9, 11, 15, 179, 182
Parent 26, 164, 169
patron 92, 93, 182
Pavlov 124, 125, 133
perception 17, 53, 58, 61, 62, 65, 136
permission 14, 43, 76, 80
asking for 14

Perrow, C. 17, 75
personnel 82, 110, 111
Peter, L. 87, 88, 95
physical conditions 24, 28, 58, 97–9, 110, 120, 127, 128, 133, 147
planning culture 9, 29, 98, 100–2, 105, 110–12, 116, 137, 159, 160, 176, 177
Potter S. 3
power 1, 3, 4, 7–18, 21, 24, 25, 27, 44, 48, 52, 53, 56–8, 60, 64–7, 71, 73, 74, 76–80, 82, 84, 90–2, 94, 97, 100, 102–6, 108, 114, 115, 120–3, 128, 134, 135, 141, 146, 153, 164, 167–9, 176, 181, 184, 185
absolute 1, 77, 102, 129, 181
achievement of 12, 15, 21, 106
gaining 1, 3, 7, 9, 10, 11, 13–15, 94, 100, 103, 114, 115, 135, 146, 184
in the organisation game 1, 3, 7, 92, 94, 97, 103, 104, 114, 115, 146, 181, 184, 185
of group 18, 44, 48, 52, 53, 57, 60, 64–7, 77, 79, 80, 90, 94, 103, 108, 121, 128, 169, 176
pursuit of 11, 12, 16, 17, 94, 146
pragmatism 136
praise 129, 134, 135
prerogative, managerial 47
proactivity 152
procedures 68, 73, 82, 86, 89, 157
process 4, 5, 15, 26–8, 32, 34, 36, 38, 41, 48, 51–4, 56, 57, 59, 67, 68, 75, 79, 82, 102–4, 117, 120, 125–33, 138, 140, 143, 145, 147–50, 155, 156, 161, 166, 167, 175, 178, 185
product, shifting 117, 139, 144, 145, 152, 155, 178
professional:
approach 41, 42, 49, 75, 82
people 17, 30, 74, 82, 84
professionalism 68
project life cycle 158–60, 177

promotion 69, 74, 87, 88, 91, 92, 103, 107, 111–14
protégés 93
Protestant work ethic 18
psyche 13, 22, 24, 25, 31, 42, 43, 108, 110, 121, 152, 176, 182
psychopathic 5, 15, 25, 26, 32, 33, 174
punishment 53, 128–34, 181

Quinn, J.B. 56

Ramussen, E. 60
rationality 31, 32, 64, 122
    see also man, rational
realities, political 103
regulations 73
Reid, J. 44, 97
reinforcement 125, 126, 130–4, 179
    positive 17, 29, 32, 41, 53, 54, 56, 59, 91, 93, 109, 116, 117, 127, 129, 130, 131–3, 152, 165–7, 179, 181, 183
relationships, interpersonal 147
retaliation 2, 183
reward 5, 18–20, 70, 99, 121, 122, 125–34, 145, 150
    see also reinforcement, positive
rewards 4, 7, 9, 13, 84, 126, 128, 132, 136, 144–6, 185
    non-material 126, 128, 132
risk adverse 86
route 12, 99, 100, 105, 110, 111, 116, 118
rules 1, 12, 14–16, 21, 26, 27, 28, 32, 34–6, 38–43, 52, 47, 67, 69, 72, 74–84, 86, 87, 89, 91, 101, 110, 114, 116, 129, 152, 168, 171, 181, 184, 185, 187
    internalising 26

Saint Francis 43
sanctions 47, 53, 69
Sappington, L.B. 162
satisfaction, partial 143
saying 'no' 14
scalar chain 74, 75, 77

Schadenfreude 31
self, inner 15, 21, 110
self-determination 15, 94
self-interest 136, 181, 182
Shaw, E. 68
Sherif, M. 57, 58
Skinner, B.F. 125, 129
social:
    development 50, 121
    needs 140, 143, 144, 147, 150
    relationship 49
socialisation 26, 28, 32, 34, 36, 69, 90
socialism 79
specialists 5, 49
spinster, Victorian 28
status 1, 4, 5, 7, 13, 34, 68, 75, 80, 84, 94, 103, 128, 147, 171, 184
stimulus 125, 126
subordinates 6, 9–12, 15, 45, 46, 48, 49, 60, 88, 101, 117, 118, 129, 135, 136, 138, 145, 147, 155, 156, 160–2, 164, 165, 167, 170, 172, 175, 179, 185
subordination of individual 27
subservience 17
sucking up 1, 182
Super Ego 22, 24, 26–36, 38, 39, 41–3, 67, 68, 72, 75, 78, 81, 84, 89, 90, 94, 95, 101, 110, 112, 121, 122, 123, 129, 134, 147, 152, 154, 161, 163, 166, 168, 173, 174, 179, 185
superiors 9–12, 15, 17, 90–2, 101, 112, 118, 182, 183, 185
survival 11, 24–7, 31, 39, 51, 52, 70, 86
synergy 71
systems people 5

Taylor, F. 19
team 2, 4, 14, 40, 48, 54, 55, 59, 121, 145, 154, 155, 157, 159–61, 163, 165–7, 172, 176–8, 180, 182
    needs 159
    spirit 59

Thatcher, M. (Baroness) 153, 163, 164
Theory X, Y 137–9, 161
time, management of 6, 7, 19, 41, 80, 83, 89, 90, 94, 100–2, 109, 111, 112, 114–16, 118, 166, 173, 179, 180
Total Quality Management (TQM) 6, 182, 184
training 4, 5, 9, 39–42, 74–6, 85, 110, 116, 130, 150, 154, 155, 166, 185
traitor within 67
Triad 22, 24–6, 28, 31, 34, 42, 43, 121–3, 134, 135
    see also Ego, Id, Super Ego

volunteering 14

wages, psychological 126–8, 148
Weber, M. 73–6, 80, 81, 86, 96, 122
Weitz, B. 129
White, R. 174, 175, 180
will 11, 15, 32, 56, 152, 183, 184
    imposing 11, 89, 103, 167, 183
winner 1, 5, 9, 14–22, 67, 85, 95, 99, 106, 109, 120, 122, 124, 135, 148, 154, 181, 182
    ways of 1, 15, 17, 20, 22, 106
wishful thinking 29, 99, 118, 121
Wolfe, J.B. 127
work:
    as an end 18
    unnecessary 18

Young, H. 165